GOLD AT LAST

GOLD AT LAST

SYLVIE FRÉCHETTE

with LILIANNE LACROIX
Translated by KATHE ROTH

Stoddart

Published in 1994 by
Stoddart Publishing Co. Limited
34 Lesmill Road
Toronto, Canada
M3B 2T6
(416) 445-3333

Reprinted August 1994

Original French edition published under the title
Sylvie Fréchette: Sans fausse note
by Les Éditions de l'Homme in 1993

Published under agreement with
Les Éditions de l'Homme, Montréal

Canadian Cataloguing in Publication Data

Fréchette, Sylvie, 1967–
Gold at last

Translation of: Sylvie Fréchette : sans fausse note.
ISBN 0-7737-5672-8

1. Fréchette, Sylvie, 1967–   .   2. Synchronized swimming.
3. Olympic Games (25th : 1992 : Barcelona, Spain).
4. Swimmers — Quebec (Province) — Biography.
I. Lacroix, Lilianne.   II. Title.

GV838.F73A313 1994   797.2′1′092   C94-931185-5

Cover photo: Canapress Photo Service (Paul Chiasson)
Typesetting: Tony Gordon Ltd.

Printed and bound in Canada

*Stoddart Publishing gratefully acknowledges the support of the
Canada Council, Ontario Ministry of Culture, Tourism, and
Recreation, Ontario Arts Council, and Ontario Publishing Centre
in the development of writing and publishing in Canada.*

To Julie

*Who believed in me from the beginning and
who gave herself body and soul to her athletes,
with whom I scaled the highest mountains
to whom I owe a million thank-yous*

Thanks, Coach!

"Karine"

To Daniel

*What more can I say to the person to whom I owe my new
direction in life, my new challenges, my new career,
to the person who gave me back my self-confidence*

Thanks, Daniel!

Sylvie

Contents

Gold at Last

Whoever said "Better late than never" must have received an Olympic gold medal a year and a half late, just like me!

A lot of wonderful things have happened to me since the original French edition of this book was published in the fall of 1993, including an exciting new career in communications.

But, emotionally, nothing will ever surpass the night in December 1993, a full sixteen months after the Barcelona Games, when I was presented with my gold medal during a big ceremony and show at the Montreal Forum. The medal had been denied me because of a judging error, which was finally overturned.

It's exciting enough to participate in an Olympics, but the thrill of receiving a medal in your own hometown defies description. It was an extraordinary evening, and for that I warmly thank Dick Pound, a fellow Montrealer and vice-president of the International Olympic Committee, who personally intervened with the IOC to ask that a full-protocol medal-presentation ceremony be held in Canada.

I also want to thank all the Canadians who supported

and encouraged me. I was never more proud to be a Canadian than when I watched the Canadian flag being raised and heard our anthem being played in the Forum.

I have received such an unbelievable cascade of tributes, honours, and support since returning from Barcelona that I must now insist on being permitted to "return the favour." My new mission is to promote Canadian amateur sports and our athletes, including the incomparable team that brought home so many medals from the Lillehammer Winter Games in February 1994. I am doing this through my job as an ambassador for the National Bank of Canada's Olympic athletes support program and as a television commentator at amateur sports events, including Lillehammer. What more could someone ask from life than to work at something she loves?

Another of my new ventures is a TV talk show in which I interview well-known people from various walks of life who have accomplished great things in the past and who continue to be successful in their new lives.

In short, although I am out of the pool after eighteen years, I continue to try to do my very best at whatever I attempt.

And that's the message I try to pass on to young people I talk to during my National Bank tours of Canada. After all, no one can demand any more than that of you.

Sylvie Fréchette
Spring 1994

Chronology

27 June 1967	Born, Rosemont
14 December 1970	Brother Martin born
11 April 1971	Father, René, dies
1979	First appearance at Canadian Junior Championships: places 23rd of 24 in duet
1981	Canadian junior champion in solo, duet, and team
1982	Canadian junior champion in solo and team
1984	Synchronized swimming becomes an Olympic sport
1985	FINA World Cup: first place in team
	Australian Games: first place in solo and duet (with Nathalie Audet)
1986	Commonwealth Games, Edinburgh: gold medal
	Meet in USSR: first in solo
1987	FINA World Cup, Cairo: second place
	Pan Am Games, Indianapolis: silver medal
1988	Excluded from Olympic Games in Seoul
	Synchro Roma, Rome: first place in solo, duet, and team
1989	(February) Soviet Women's Magazine Competition, Moscow: first place in solo
	(May) Canadian senior champion in solo
	(June) Majorca Synchro: first place in solo
	World Cup, Paris: second place in solo, third

place in duet (with Nathalie Guay), second place in team. Last duet championship. Until the 1992 Olympic Games in Barcelona, Sylvie is not defeated again.

1990

(January) Commonwealth Games, Auckland, New Zealand: gold medal in solo. One judge gives Sylvie a perfect mark.

(April) Loano Cup, Italy: first place in solo

(May) Canadian senior champion in solo

(June) Roma Synchro: first place in solo

(July) Swiss Open, Lancy: first place in solo

(November) German Open: first place in solo

1991

(January) World Championships, Perth, Australia: gold medal in solo (world record in cumulative score)

(May) Canadian senior champion in solo

World cup, Bonn: first place in solo

(July) Swiss Open, Liechtenstein: first place in solo

Roma Synchro: first place in solo

(September) Pre-Olympic competition: first place in solo

(November) International competition, Brno, Czechoslovakia: first place in solo

1992

(March) German Open: first place in solo

(April) Canadian senior champion in solo

(May) Japan Synchro: first place in solo

Roma Synchro: first place in solo

(23 June–15 July) Training camp in Puerto Rico

(16–17 July) Trip to Toronto to introduce Olympic team

(18 July) Sylvain Lake dies. He was to leave for Barcelona that evening.

Barcelona

(22 July) Sylvie leaves for Barcelona

Olympic Games

(25 July) Opening ceremonies for Barcelona
Olympic Games; Sylvain's funeral in Montreal

(2 August) Preliminaries: Sylvie is tied with
American Kristen Babb

(5 August) Compulsory figures: due to an error
by the Brazilian judge, Sylvie is in fourth place,
when she should have been in first

(6 August) Solo final: Sylvie wins the final but
places second in combined marks; silver medal
in solo

PROLOGUE

"Karine" Fréchette

G*o for it, girl! Besides the 11,000 people up in the stands, the whole world is watching you. Impress every one of those millions of people! Even the ones who didn't want to give you the score you deserved in compulsory figures and who could cost you the Olympic gold medal. Especially them. Make sure they regret it! Show them what it takes to be a world champion . . .*

It's funny. For years I've been telling myself that I'm the best, and for years I've tried hard to believe it. But in fact, the real swimmer, the champion synchronized swimmer, is Karine. I know that better than anyone.

Her name is Karine, Karine Fréchette. She's been there from the beginning, like a twin sister somewhere inside me. Officially, Karine came into being because there were too many girls named Sylvie at the Georges-Vernot pool, where all of us CAMO (Club Aquatique Montréal Olympique) synchronized swimmers trained, and there were terrible mix-ups with the underwater microphone.

"Turn right, Sylvie," Julie Sauvé, my one and only coach,

would shout, and three or four of us, heads in the water, would turn right.

So we decided to give some swimmers new names. Grandmother Fréchette, who was also my godmother, was called Corinne. The other girls thought the name was a little old-fashioned, so we updated it and I became Karine. On the outside was a nice, slightly shy, very ordinary young girl; on the inside was Karine, the stubborn athlete. Without her, no one would ever have heard of me. Without her, Sylvie Fréchette would have been known only to friends and family.

All champions have the soul of a competitor, a steel-strong alter ego that emerges in difficult moments and pushes them beyond what they ever thought possible. At CAMO, because of a little technical problem, we went even farther: we named our alter egos. Catherine Paradis, one of my first duet partners, was Annie. Nathalie Guay, my last partner, was Natou. And I was Karine — in the water, and on land, when I needed her.

Even today, it's Karine who pushes me beyond my limits. She's the one who came up with the idea for this book. An autobiography by a twenty-five-year-old seemed ridiculous to me. So, Karine's little voice whispered, why not tell *my* story?

When I began to laugh, I knew Karine had won. Again.

I've always loved to laugh. Silly, spontaneous laughter, just like that, for no reason really — because I feel good, because I'm happy, or to make up for all the times when I cried over the slightest little thing. With the Olympic Games in Barcelona, 1992 should have been the perfect year. *My* year. Instead, it was a year from hell. First, my grandfather died, then Sylvain. (But I mustn't think about that, especially that.) And then, when the Brazilian judge made that mistake punching in her score, costing me the gold medal, it was the last straw. What more could happen to me?

Swim, Sylvie! Next movement . . . Wow, great! Later, we'll check the video to see whether that tiny space you wanted between your legs

*was visible. Push a little harder. Soon, very soon, you'll be able to get
a breath of fresh air.*

Until then, everything was going pretty well. The beginning of my program at the edge of the pool, which always
made me so nervous, went without a hitch. When you're lying
on your stomach, balancing on one rib and one knee with
your arms touching the water, it isn't exactly easy to feel in
control. But in a sport where artistic impression counts so
much, you do what you have to do. All the same, God, I was
scared! Despite all the hours of training, I was sure that I'd
fall to pieces under the pressure and make a fool of myself in
front of the whole world.

Finally, this endless moment passed; as soon as I felt the
water around me, I was back in my element. I think I must
have been a dolphin in another life. On land, I've always felt
too tall, too fat or too thin, awkward, and a bit insignificant,
but in the water, I've always had the feeling that no one could
be more comfortable than me — or rather, Karine.

I had decided that my hairstyle would be different for
this Olympic final. Instead of the usual little bun, I wanted a
French braid. Actually, the idea was completely crazy. It might
have been okay if we'd tried it before Barcelona, but we
hadn't! On the other hand, it broke with convention, and
both Julie and I liked it. As for Karine, there was no question.
"Go for it," she urged. "It's all or nothing!" Actually, the braid
would go well with the Vangelis music for my solo final and
would help create the effect I wanted of a religious cult
experience, something like the sacrifice of a virgin to the
gods.

Since no one on the team knew how to do French braids,
I went to the Olympic Village hairdresser, a well-meaning
woman who spoke only Spanish and didn't know a thing
about synchronized swimming. We tried to explain it to her:
synchronized swimming, with a girl moving around in the
water, is nothing like a fashion show or a gala affair: the

hairdo absolutely has to hold. But she didn't get the message. After the preliminaries, her skilful work was so loose that it was about to come undone. If something like this were to happen in competition, it would spell disaster. The deductions for artistic impression, which can be drastic if even a single strand of hair is out of place, would be severe.

Just before the competition, Denise, Julie's sister and CAMO's head coach, decided to take charge. She undid the even looser braid made by a second hairdresser we had found that morning, then redid it, carefully following the same style, but making it much tighter and using lots of hair gel.

I couldn't have asked Julie to do my hair again. Since the error in scoring during the compulsories, she had been running all over the place, seeking explanations, registering our protest and then our appeal, trying to get justice. She was working on my behalf, and I had to give her the freedom to do it. Anyway, Denise was dependable, and could stay calm no matter how much excitement was swirling around. Indeed, the braid she made held up well.

Pull your shoulders in. Push your legs to the right. Tighten your bum . . .

The swimsuit, too, had to be original, and it had to fit the choreography. I wanted to look like a young bride, so the top part was made of lace. No swimmer had ever worn lace. We weren't sure how the officials would react, but nothing in the rules forbade it. If a world champion couldn't do something new, who could?

As usual, Pauline, a family friend, was in charge of decorating the white swimsuit. But the first time I jumped in the water wearing it, for a photo session in Toronto a few days before leaving for the Games, the sparkling rhinestones came unglued. It was a hilarious scene: as the cameras flashed, the rhinestones dropped to the edge of the pool one by one, "clink, clink, clink . . ." Here was the world champion, falling apart before your very eyes!

The evening before I left for Barcelona, my mother and my aunts all gathered in our kitchen to sew rhinestones and pearls onto the Lycra and lace. When it was finished, my uncles wanted to watch the fashion show. To get me in the mood and create a sort of disco ambience while I paraded in front of them, they flicked the lights on and off. Then they applauded, and we all roared with laughter.

My mother, my brother, Martin, and the rest of my family have always been there for me.

ONE

The Wise Old Man

Mom, I know you're sitting up there somewhere in the crowd. But where? I'd feel so much better if I could see you . . .

It's strange. Every journalist who's ever written about me has said that I'm an orphan, as though that would add lustre to my medals. In fact, what they should have said was that my mother was a widow and that despite the hardships, which she never let anyone see, she always did her very best to be both father and mother to Martin and me.

Poor Mom. I wasn't even four years old and Martin was a tiny baby when Papa died.

It was a car accident. René Fréchette was on his way to his shift as a bus driver at dawn when a drunk driver crashed into his car in the "tunnel of death" at the corner of St. Joseph and Iberville in Montreal. When the doorbell rang, I ran to answer it, all proud because I was finally tall enough to reach the button that opened the door, one floor below, leading to our apartment. When I saw the policemen, I was scared. I thought that all the police did was arrest robbers.

To give Mom a little time to herself, her brothers took

me with them when they went to see the car. They didn't
realize then that a three-year-old soaks up words like a
sponge. For years after, I "explained" the accident to Mom,
including every detail my uncles could have imagined and
describing every image of the twisted vehicle burned into my
memory. Every once in a while, using my toy cars and dolls,
I re-enacted the tragedy.

The driver who caused the accident learned what he'd
done from the newspapers. He walked away from it with a
sprained thumb. As for the "tunnel of death," it is still there,
claiming its share of victims.

I have almost no memories of my father, just a few mental
snapshots, like the one where he's standing on a ladder
putting up a poster of Bobino that I wanted on the ceiling
right above my bed. My memories come mostly from Mom,
who reminds us every April 24 that it's his birthday and tells
us how old he would have been.

Whenever I left for a competition, Mom would tell me that
Papa would help me breathe. It's the only thing I would ask as
I started my program: "Breathe for me." I hoped that it would
ease the obsession that tortures all synchronized-swimming
competitors. Papa's breath, coming from heaven, was perhaps a little stronger than my own.

Mom kept Papa's memory alive, holding back the emptiness that his death could have brought. Nevertheless, we
were almost penniless, and Mom moved us into an apartment
above her parents', which reduced our expenses considerably. She knew how to make fun out of nothing; in her hands,
for instance, humble Jell-O became a feast.

Christmas was coming. The previous summer, I'd fallen
in love. I had seen him at the store with the other stuffed toys,
and I had named him Chiquita. He was a little brown monkey,
exactly like the dozen others around him. Mom let me hold
him while we were shopping, but I had to put him back on
his shelf before we went to the checkout counter. Every week,

one of the monkeys disappeared. One day, it was all over; they were all gone, and other plush animals had taken their place. I didn't say anything; I didn't even cry as I usually did and still do over the least little thing.

On Christmas day, after opening boxes full of funny trinkets, I found Chiquita. The last monkey on the shelf had been mine.

My Chiquita! For there was absolutely no doubt that he was mine. Mom, an excellent seamstress who made my bed-spreads and curtains as well as my clothes, had dressed him in a red T-shirt with the CAMO logo on the back, in honour of my swimming club. From that day on, Chiquita was my good-luck charm at competitions.

Every summer we went to the cottage at Notre-Dame-de-la-Merci. Grandpa Charbonneau and my uncles had built it when I was learning to walk. Bare-chested, the men nailed, sawed, and sweated while Mom followed me like a shadow to keep me from tripping all over the construction site. This lakeside cottage was my beloved grandfather's domain and a retreat for the entire family.

When I was older and anyone asked who my hero was, I always laughed and said Flipper, the dolphin on the TV show. To tell the truth, though, it was Grandpa.

I never once heard him raise his voice or swear. When he spoke, in his usual soft tones, everyone stopped to listen. My mother's contagious capacity for marvelling at things, for making a simple shopping trip into an intense experience, surely came from her father.

I would ask my mother, "Cuddle me," and she would lie on my bed, stroking my hair gently and talking softly.

I would ask my grandfather, "Grandpa, tell me about . . ." And, as we walked down the dirt road, in the black of night, he would tell me about the stars and show me how the moon never came up in the same place twice.

All summer long, we would chase frogs and build houses

for them. Everything that crawled or jumped made us happy. One particular summer, Nadia Comaneci was dazzling crowds with her brilliance at the Summer Olympics in Montreal, but I remained in blissful ignorance of Olympic fever, busy with my frogs . . .

Even in winter, the cottage was a continual source of adventures. With my uncle Jean-Marie, we built a log cabin from an old, dead fir tree we found in the woods. This became *our* house. A hole in the snow served as our kitchen; we would light a fire there and roast hot dogs. Martin sometimes dressed up as a soldier and stood guard over our territory.

Everything at the cottage was marvellous. One summer, rain kept us inside for four days and we ran out of things to do. Finally, when the downpour let up, we invented a game based on the TV show *Le petit castor*. Dressed in rubber boots and K-Ways, we tramped through the woods without following the paths. Like the little beaver on TV, we were off to discover nature. Suddenly, we stumbled upon the most beautiful clearing in the world. Sunbeams wove their way through the branches, catching the drops of water clinging to the leaves. Water trickled down tree trunks and through the moss. There was water streaming everywhere, and it sparkled, sparkled, sparkled. We were absolutely sure we had discovered paradise.

The next day, we wanted to go back and see it again. Our clearing was there, all right, but the magic wasn't: the spot had become drab, ordinary. Nothing sparkled anymore. Our paradise had lasted but one day.

To keep us amused, Grandpa set up an eight-hole golf course around the house. The loser wiped the dishes. Since I had no talent for golf, I was often the one wiping the dishes while Grandpa washed as he hummed an old ballad. He was the official dishwasher; he was also quite often the cook.

His specialty was *chiard*, as he called it: a sort of giblet stew that neither looked nor tasted particularly appetizing, but which we both wolfed down with gusto. We were the only ones who appreciated *chiard*. Grandma, who found it appalling that he would serve such a concoction to children and who wouldn't have eaten it for all the gold in the world, forbade him to make it for us. So he would wait until she and my mother were out, usually shopping in the village, then whisper conspiratorially in my ear, "How about cooking up some *chiard*?" Now that I think about it, it wouldn't surprise me if Grandma, who adored her husband, sometimes got out of the house on purpose to leave us to our little forbidden, but innocent, pleasures. For everyone wanted to please Grandpa. Especially me!

Although I loved *chiard*, I wouldn't have minded if another of Grandpa's specialties had disappeared from the menu forever. It's funny, each of his dishes seemed to have its particular context. The *chiard* was for the cottage. Pan-fried sausages with canned corn was for home, when he came to babysit Martin and me. How I detested that dish! But I always swallowed the sausages happily, with an ear-to-ear smile, for I wouldn't have hurt Grandpa for anything in the world. Now that he's gone, I never eat a single bite of sausage.

From time to time, so that our stays in the country wouldn't affect my training too much, he would encourage me to keep in shape. "Go on, my dear, swim across the lake," he'd say, or he'd tell me to go for a run.

One day, when I was out jogging, I saw a little fox. At first, I stood stock still, sure that he'd run away. But he just stood there not showing the slightest trace of fear. He was quite small, but I turned and ran back to the house as if the devil were at my heels. When I saw him prowling around the house that evening, I panicked. He'd followed me; now, I was sure, he would bite me, devour me.

But my grandfather put his arm around my shoulders and said, "Look how thin he is. Come on, let's help him."

Every day after that I had a mission: to catch a fish for

my fox. We'd wrap the fish in aluminum foil, and when we heard it crinkle we knew we had a visitor. The fox came more and more often.

July arrived, and with it the construction holiday. The cottages filled up, but the little fox still came faithfully. Then, one day, when he ventured onto the property of a neighbouring cottage, someone took a rifle and shot him. That guy was probably scared of foxes, too, and likely didn't have a grandfather to tell him about them . . .

In November 1991, Grandpa received a letter from the government. They were taking away his driver's licence. Three weeks earlier, his physician had examined him and recommended that he not drive at night. But now they were taking his licence away entirely. No more licence meant no more cottage, and the cottage was his life. Grandpa, my big grandpa, who always enjoyed his food and drink, stopped eating entirely.

I had been world champion since the beginning of the year, and I was well known. If I couldn't help Grandpa, what was any of it worth? I had to do something. So I put on my Team Canada jacket, and Grandma, Grandpa, and I went off to the ophthalmologist. Surely there had been a mistake; after all, the doctor had only mentioned limiting Grandpa's night driving, nothing else.

We'll never know what changed the government's mind: a new eye exam, my grandfather's state of utter despair, perhaps my Team Canada jacket. In any case, Grandpa got his licence back, but some spark in him had died, as if he had just discovered that he was old.

A few months before the Olympics, Grandpa was up at the cottage and decided to go snowshoeing on the short trail. Grandma was in the middle of washing the dishes, and she told him to go ahead, that she would catch up to him soon.

When Grandpa opened the door, Blandy bolted outside. Blandy was Grandpa's dog, a big chow chow that ate from his hand and acknowledged no other master. Worried that the dog might scare the neighbours, Grandpa ran out to catch him without even stopping to strap on his snowshoes. He had to hurry. The dog was already at the edge of the frozen lake . . .

A bit later, when she opened the door to go and join him, Grandma found Grandpa lying at the bottom of the stairs, with Blandy licking his blue-tinged face. Grandma, a tiny woman, couldn't even move him.

The entire family gathered in Grandpa's apartment. Good times and bad, we always stuck together.

Once before, a few years earlier, we had all gathered to cry together. Jean-François, my young cousin, had died. The grown-ups sighed or wept, but we children were stunned. We all knew that Jean-François wasn't healthy, that he was frail, but how could he die? Children didn't die!

With Grandpa's death, all those questions with no answers returned. It was a nightmare, and I would surely wake up. It wasn't possible that such a horrible thing could have taken place at the cottage. Not at the cottage! Nothing bad happens in paradise, and the cottage was my paradise — it was everyone's paradise. Moreover, Grandpa had been in excellent shape, in spite of his seventy-eight years. How could he die that way? And there was one question above all that tortured me. The Olympic Games were coming. Why now, Grandpa? Why didn't you wait? You would have been so proud to see me.

For years, he and Grandma had gone from pool to pool to see me swim. My big grandpa would suffer from the heat, but he refused to step outside for even a minute to get some fresh air in case he'd miss me. And now he was going to miss the biggest moment of my career. Grandpa!

At the funeral home, I broke down. They had to tear him from my arms so that they could close the casket. Where was Karine, that strong girl who knew how to keep her dignity through anything, now?

With no master, Blandy began to act mean and stopped eating. Finally, he had to be put to sleep. He didn't want to live without his master. But how were all of us going to live without Grandpa?

TWO

The Beanpole

Go for it, Sylvie! Just a few more minutes and it will be all over . . .
You've never swum so well; it's as if you're walking on water.

Just before I jumped into the pool for the Olympic final, I
looked my coach Julie Sauvé straight in the eye and said, "I
hate being nervous like this. I've always hated it. But you know
what? When it's all over, after this last solo, that's what I'll miss
the most."

In fact, I felt like I'd managed to calm my nerves. The
American, Kristen Babb, who had gone just before me, had
used country music. Never, ever could I have swum to music
like that. But while I was preparing for my turn to jump into
the water, the lively music was perfect. For years, people had
called me "grasshopper" because of my habit of hopping up
and down before I competed. It's my way of warming up. At
that moment, exhilarated by the country music, I started
dancing, hopping from foot to foot and turning in all directions. I'd never felt so crazy. Denise and Julie took pictures of
me and of my feet, and we laughed till we cried. But in spite
of my dancing, in spite of the pictures, in spite of our wild

laughter, nerves, those horrible nerves that twisted my gut, would grab me again in an instant.

As always, as soon as I hit the water the fear disappeared. Oh, it felt good to have the water around me.

As far back as I can remember, water has always washed away my troubles, let me empty my mind when the pain was too great. In the water, Karine takes over. Gone is Mom's little girl; Julie's girl, stronger, cooler, takes over.

It was because of the cottage, because the lake was so near, that my mother decided to sign me up for swimming lessons. I was a natural swimmer, but I couldn't dive because I was scared, so the others laughed at me. Still, I was unbeatable in the water, and they called me "the motor." Sylvain, whose sister Josée was the world amputee swimming champion, sometimes came to the pool. He once told me that he remembered me from then: "You were the beanpole who didn't know how to dive but won all the races anyway." We laughed . . . But I don't want to think about him, about that.

At any rate, swimming suited me better than most other activities. For example, at one time I wanted to be a majorette, and so I joined the Montreal Olympics for a few months. In spite of their grandiose name, they weren't a very strong team and always came in last or second-last in official competitions. But I was even worse: I was so bad that I was constantly hitting myself with the baton. That year, against all expectations, our club was invited to the Quebec Carnaval. Only fifty could go, and there were fifty-three of us. I was left home. I definitely had more of a future as a swimmer.

One day, in a corner of the pool, I noticed some girls who were managing to keep their arms out of the water without sinking. To me, it looked like magic! They told me that it was synchronized swimming.

When I heard that they needed girls to put on a show, I signed up. Then came competitions. We didn't always win. One team in particular struck fear in our hearts: we didn't like those girls much because whenever they were competing, we could say goodbye to our gold-medal chances. I dubbed them with a rather unoriginal nickname: "the Black Swimsuits."

Soon, our club folded. Someone suggested that I join CAMO, which also offered swimming and "synchro" lessons. After a few weeks, I switched once and for all to synchronized swimming. I had been training for several weeks with the club at the Georges-Vernot pool when I competed for the first time with my new team. That's when I found out that I was with the Black Swimsuits.

Every afternoon after school, I left for the bus stop with my enormous, ugly bag with blue flowers printed on it. From the balcony, Mom and Martin waved goodbye.

At that time, CAMO had only two coaches, not nine, as there are now. Julie was in charge of the little kids like me.

Little, in a manner of speaking. My friends didn't even come up to my shoulder. I was so tall for my age that my mother had to show my birth certificate to squelch the ugly, insulting rumour that she was lying about my age. As for me, I didn't know what to do with myself. In photographs, I hid behind everyone, my back hunched and my knees bent so that I wouldn't stick out. How I hated myself!

I soaked up synchro like a sponge. Little by little, I dropped competitive swimming and began to concentrate on synchro, even though I knew that brothers Tom and Dave Johnson, the coaches at the Pointe-Claire club, wanted me to race for their team. I think Julie was keeping an eye on me. I was such an ugly duckling, but she must have seen something promising in me, perhaps precisely in those long legs that embarrassed me so much.

I fell in love with Julie at first sight. She was so pretty and so funny, and she always made us laugh. At the time, she wore wonderful shoes with very high silver heels that seemed not to be attached to anything. Above them, the delicate uppers looked like they were floating. She never knew it, but we nicknamed those shoes "Cosmos." We never could figure out how they were held together, but were we impressed!

I was such an awkward beanpole, I could never be so elegant.

She only got angry once. Some girls had been acting mean to me and they had relegated me to a corner of the locker room, which they named, after me, "long-legs corner."

"If Sylvie wins, it's because of her long legs . . ." they'd mutter.

The day she heard that, Julie got good and mad. "She's the same age as you," she reprimanded them. "You'll all grow, too. If she wins, it's because she works very hard."

She called it working. If she only knew . . . I was having so much fun, and I wanted to do so well. Painfully shy away from the pool, in the water I wanted all of Julie's attention:

"Julie, Julie, look! I think I got it!"

"Julie, is it like this or like that?"

"Julie! Julie!"

I *was* a bit of a nuisance and stubborn. It wasn't just my long legs that annoyed my teammates. But after Julie's outburst everything changed. The tension disappeared, and I took my place in the locker room alongside the other girls.

We invented a game. Every evening, we threw our clothes in a big, messy heap in the middle of the locker room. We called it "making a cake." Then, on a signal, we threw ourselves on the pile to dig out the articles of clothing that belonged to us. The first one dressed was the winner.

How we laughed among those grey lockers! But never like the time that we were putting together a show and trying to think up new arm movements, new positions, leg movements. One of us ran to get Julie. "Come quick, Julie! We've thought up a new routine."

Julie opened the door and froze on the spot. She stood there speechless, torn between wanting to scold us or laugh as she stared at us, all "synchronized" but naked as jaybirds, half hidden by the doors of our lockers and dancing to the disco beat of "Funky Town!"

I thought of the pool as my second home. But Mom had laid down the law: swimming must come after schoolwork. When I was in fourth grade, I once got a mark that was a little lower than usual — in English, I think. When I got home from school, I was crying so hard that Mom didn't know what to do, until she figured out that I thought she wouldn't let me go swimming. "Poor baby," she said, stroking my hair.

Gradually my training increased from a few hours a week to five hours a day.

My brother, Martin, had never played any sport. Or, rather, he tried everything once or twice. Whenever it got serious, he would quit, as if he was scared of getting caught in the cogs of a big machine.

His friends came and looked, rather enviously, at my medals hanging one behind the other on the curtain rod. But Martin shook his head when he saw me come home, night after night, with wet hair and an empty stomach. By the time I sat down to eat supper and then do my homework at one end of the table, it had been dark outside for hours. He must have thought I was crazy. Even today, I'm sure he thinks I haven't lived, because I didn't have a childhood or adolescence. It's strange: sometimes I feel like I'm fifty years old, while at other times, in other ways, I feel like I'm still a little girl. Perhaps Martin isn't so wrong after all.

But if I had it to do all over again, I'd do the same thing without the slightest hesitation. I loved swimming so much. But I know that seeing me rushing so much, swimming and having no time for anything else, turned Martin off competitive sport. In a way, it's too bad. He would have done well at any sport he tried.

THREE

Buddha, the Prince, and Gana

Barcelona. It's great to swim feeling the sun on my skin like this . . .
It's a change from indoor pools. But, for me, Barcelona is also the
end of the ride.

There were lots of trips, and Julie always found a way to spice
them up. If we went to a competition in Rome or Japan, she'd
add two or three days to the stay by finding such advantageous
fares that no one would have thought of refusing. "It's crazy
going so far just to see pools," she would say.

Travelling was the reward, the compensation for the
year's efforts. But why Julie prolonged her own agony by
accompanying her band of unruly schoolchildren, I'll never
know. The first time we went to Japan, in 1984, we were all
very excited. Once, we followed a Japanese woman dressed
in traditional garb down the street. At first surprised and a
little scared, the beautiful woman finally let us take her
picture as she twirled her parasol and smiled for us.

There were, however, less happy moments. Unable to
immerse ourselves in the holy ambience that reigned in a
sanctuary, we took pictures of one another sitting in the lotus

position in front of a giant Buddha. It turned out that we were immortalizing our utter lack of tact. The looks of the Japanese people around us should have made us realize that we were bordering on sacrilege.

Everything was an excuse to have fun. When we were invited to a typical Japanese restaurant by the Canadian consul in Tokyo, some of us made a vow: we would eat whatever food was served to us. The short walk through the dark neighbourhood where the restaurant was located, and the geishas strumming their guitars, put us in the mood.

Unfortunately, we never promised to be polite. Our cries of "Ugh!" accompanied the presentation of every dish, until they brought out the most shocking dish of all. On our way into the restaurant, we had stopped to look at the little crabs crawling around in the aquarium. They were so funny. But when we saw them on our plates, covered in batter and staring at us with their round, incredulous eyes, we were flabbergasted. Oh, no, not that!

But a promise was a promise. We looked at one another: "One, two, three, go!" Each of us making sure she wasn't the first, we popped them into our mouths and began chewing. They tasted salty, a little like potato chips. After that, we ordered bowls of fried crabs every evening in our rooms.

It was shortly after the Los Angeles Olympic Games, so we were the only club team participating in the international competition, which had brought together some of the strongest national teams in the world. We were a little nervous, but we had our excuses. Of course, we were very young, but above all, we'd been treated like celebrities since we'd gotten off the plane.

Completely unknown at home, although famous in synchronized-swimming circles, we suddenly had the heady feeling that we were rock stars. We were very surprised to find out that our little club team was the heavy favourite in the competition.

People tore off our lapel pins and our little flags and shoved each other aside to take our picture. All over the city, huge posters advertised the competition. In the subway, we found ourselves face-to-face with ourselves.

For some time, we'd been perfecting a new move: we all stayed underwater, and seven of us lifted Martine Labelle out of the water. Martine looked like she was literally floating on air. It was completely new, revolutionary, and really impressed the public and the judges. Seeing herself on the poster in the subway, Martine couldn't resist — she took it down to keep as a souvenir. Our families and friends would have had a hard time believing us.

Maybe it was because we were so pumped up, but we won the competition. Julie wept with joy. In the stands, people threw us their t-shirts, making signs that they wanted us to autograph them.

But when we came home, we had to search long and hard to find a single line about us in the papers.

I never went unnoticed in Japan. Not because of synchronized swimming, but because I was a foreigner and so tall — and blond, to boot! We usually stayed in the very chic New Otani Hotel, even in recent years, and took full advantage of being treated like princesses. One year in particular, we would gather every evening in one of the rooms and dance on the beds to Madonna singing "Starlight" on the TV. The day we left, Julie was apoplectic. Madonna had been available to us on a private pay channel, and our little dances had raised by more than five hundred dollars the bill that was graciously being paid by our Japanese hosts. Although the room was free, we had to pay this bill. As always, Julie got out of it.

Dear New Otani! The last time I went to Japan, I was quite annoyed. Instead of our usual lodgings, we were put up at a hotel that was comfortable but had tiny rooms. Julie had a good laugh at my expense: my feet extended beyond the

end of the bed, and I couldn't close the door to the bath-
room; we would have had to amputate my legs for me to fit.
I also had problems at the pool, to the point that my routine
had to be altered because my head kept hitting the bottom.
Sometimes it's not easy being 1.77 metres tall in Tokyo.

As if she hadn't had enough of our shenanigans in Japan
and to reward us for our victory on our first trip, Julie
arranged a stopover in Hawaii. Sand, blue sky, sea . . . Once
again, Julie had found a bargain fare.

When we arrived at our Maui hotel, it was almost dark.
The rooms seemed fine, and we were so tired that we went
straight to sleep, our noses buried in our pillows. When we
woke up in the morning, one of the girls opened the curtain
and let out a yell. Soon we were all in Julie's room, complaining, crying, wanting to go home.

There was no sand and no sunbathers in front of the
hotel. We were across from the harbour, in the middle of a
shabby neighbourhood. The beaches, the paradise we had
expected, were on the other side of the island, dozens of
kilometres away.

Julie rented a car and drove off.

A few hours later, the group moved to one of the most
luxurious hotels in Hawaii. Buoyed by our victory in Japan,
Julie had made her case to the manager: the girls had just
won an international competition and would give a free show,
if only there were a couple of free rooms somewhere. We
settled in to a magnificent suite . . .

We slept five to a room. To fit everyone in, we pushed
the double beds together, and each of us took a turn sleeping
on the crack. Every night was a giggle fest.

Natou, among others, gave us a good laugh, although we
had to hold ourselves back. Poor Natou! At the time, all the
girls wanted to have blond hair. Even Natou, who was so
pretty, and so brunette. Julie offered to help her "lighten"
her hair. Generous as usual, she wasn't content to follow the

directions and use just a few drops. She emptied the whole bottle onto Natou's hair, declaring, "You'll see, you'll get lighter, my girl." And she sure did. When we got back to Montreal, her own mother didn't recognize her.

The hotel manager never made us give the show Julie had promised, but he let it be known that we were staying there. From time to time, tourists would see us executing moves as we swam and ask us to pose with them in our show costumes. We had just swum to "New York, New York," for which we wore "tuxedo" swimsuits with a black belt. People found them funny, and so did we.

Yes, Julie always fought for her girls, even if the results weren't always well-advised. Just ask Mrs. Vilagos, the mother of twins Penny and Vicky. When we were at the Trevi fountain in Rome the poor lady, our lone chaperone, didn't know where to turn as she tried to chase away the forward Italians who had attached themselves to our startled, giggling group. A bunch of young girls and just one woman guarding them — what a bargain!

Sometimes, our travels took us to places that looked just like postcards. In Egypt, for instance, the people at the embassy invited us to go horseback riding. With the desert and the pyramids, this was too tempting an offer to turn down. I clung to the saddle blanket and lay on the horse's neck, my eyes closed. From time to time, I looked up: a desert sunset with a caravan in the distance. If only I could have sat up straight, I might have passed for a female Indiana Jones.

Every once in a while, I would see something that brought me back to reality: at the base of the pyramids, people were living in the middle of the cemetery in emptied crypts, among their dead. One day, they would join their ancestors quietly, without anyone noticing. Egypt was this, too.

But we weren't there just as tourists. Egypt also meant competition, and it meant different ways of doing things, which sometimes made us feel like fish out of water. For example, the Egyptians disinfected their pools with ozone instead of chlorine. It had the same effect, except for one small detail: ozone leaves green stains on the skin, at least in certain spots. The insides of our ears, our eyelids, our scalps, and the white skin between our breasts had a greenish tint. A little more and we would have looked like a bunch of Incredible Hulks.

The Americans, as green-tinted as we were, won the team competition, and we had to resign ourselves to the silver medal. During the awards ceremony, the Egyptian organizers, obviously not familiar with the Canadian flag, raised it upside down. No, such things don't happen just at baseball games, and the Toronto Blue Jays, World Series champions, were not the first to suffer this indignity!

One of the most coveted trips was the almost annual pilgrimage to the realm of Prince Rainier. Every year, we were invited to perform in Monaco during the international swimming competition. That was the good life. Immense tables, loaded down with dishes that would please the palate of the most discerning gourmet, free-flowing champagne. And no pressure in the pool, since it was just an exhibition. On top of that, we had fun ogling the handsome swimmers around us.

It was in Monaco that I saw American swimmer Matt Biondi for the first time. He was so tall — 1.95 metres — his shoulders so broad, and his body so superb that he looked like a god, and he was just as inaccessible. Like teenagers swooning over a rock star, we were all happy just to catch a glimpse of him, to dream, and to avail ourselves of other pleasures.

Of course, no trip to Monaco would be complete without stopping in at the casino. But you had to be twenty-five to get in, and we were just eighteen or nineteen.

"At home, we'd be old enough, Julie," we pleaded. "Come on, let's go."

Julie hesitated, but finally gave in. "All right, girls, we'll give it a try."

For three days, we plotted our attack. On the chosen evening, we put on our make-up, did our hair . . . but when we got to the casino, we almost lost our nerve. All those luxury cars parked outside — Ferraris, Mercedes, Rolls Royces — were very intimidating.

To increase our chances, we decided to go in one at a time, each trying to mix in with a group of people. Rebuffed by the doorman, some went back a second time, holding their heads down, and the most brazen tried yet again. I slipped in between two gentlemen. Doubtless because of my height, I got in on the very first try. But once I was in the casino's cold, stilted ambience, I felt quite uncomfortable. And what if they noticed me? Scared of being kicked out, I decided to leave. Karine was nowhere to be found that day. It was the others who told me that Julie won three hundred dollars at a slot machine.

Monaco also meant Prince Rainier. Unlike his daughters, who seemed a little distant, the prince always seemed to be a model of graciousness and affability. Every year, to celebrate the end of the meet, he organized an enormous party. One time, the orchestra was playing a slow tune when, charming as always, he approached our table and, bowing gallantly, asked one of the girls to dance.

Nathalie Roy is a lovely person, but nothing or no one in the world can force her to do something when she doesn't want to. Dancing with a prince didn't mean a thing to her. She turned him down!

If Julie's eyes could shoot bullets, Nathalie would have dropped dead on the spot. Poor Julie, who was so pleased to provide this trip to her girls year after year. What if our host was offended by this refusal? But, no! The next year, the good prince, sovereign of his small kingdom, invited us again.

When we were travelling, Julie was everything to us:

mother, friend, coach, and tour guide. When she wasn't there, I felt quite abandoned. In 1986, I was the only Canadian competitor sent to a meet in Moscow. Obviously, Julie had to stay at the club with the other girls. Only "Mary Poppins" went with me. Mary Poppins was Mary Ann Reeves, the technical director of Synchro Canada. I had nicknamed her because of her multicoloured jewellery, big hats, and friendly extravagance.

They had warned me that she would bring a ton of luggage, but I didn't believe it. After all, we were only going for a few days. When I saw her suitcases, I couldn't believe my eyes. Dear Mary Poppins!

"Sylvie," she asked, "can you take care of the luggage, please?"

Alone with me in Moscow, Mary Poppins had three roles: official, judge — and coach, when she had the time. It followed quite naturally that I had two roles: athlete and porter.

During training, I felt very alone. Overwhelmed with her other duties, Mary Poppins had no time left over for me. It was very hard. If I was leaning to the right or the left, I couldn't tell. If only I had had a video camera . . . Without a coach or video, I oriented myself according to the lights set into the walls.

But there were difficulties at every turn. When it was time for the compulsories, the officials announced the figures to be performed — in Russian. I saw the Americans turn to the interpreter who was accompanying them. But what had he told them, for God's sake? I watched them train for a few minutes. Good, there was an "albatross." And, yes, another figure. In the end, I figured it out. I'd been competing for a while, and fortunately I had gained some experience. In fact, I was already considered to be among the best in the world.

Nevertheless, once the competition was over, I couldn't say how I'd managed to get by. The calculations were so complex, and the marks so close . . .

When I got on the bus after the compulsories, the other swimmers came to say hi, even the Americans. They all said the same thing, in English: "Congratulations." I was a little puzzled.

At the time, my English was almost as limited as my Russian, and I didn't really know what was going on. I was reading quietly in my hotel room when Mary Poppins arrived with the same word on her lips. When she showed me the results, I finally understood: I'd won the compulsories.

This trip had other surprises in store for me. Surrounded by young swimmers chatting in Russian, I was starting to do my make-up when Gana arrived.

"Bonjour!"

I looked around. The girl who had spoken was as tall as me. It was Gana Maximova, a Moscovite who spoke French a little slowly but very correctly. "Did you see me swim?" she asked.

There were dozens of swimmers competing. When I admitted that I hadn't noticed her, Gana's eyes filled with tears: "If I don't do well enough here, I won't be able to swim for my country anymore."

Her mother was her coach. Her brother swam, too, and her father worked with the Moscow circus.

Gana must have been good enough that day, since she was at the World Aquatic Championships a little later. At the World Cup some time after that, she was even chosen to swim a duet. Then she became a formidable competitor. But she wasn't at Barcelona. I didn't know why. When I thought about it, we hadn't seen her mother at a competition for some time either. I received a few letters from Paris; perhaps they had moved there.

For years, we wrote to each other. She always enclosed a little something with her letters: a calendar, a postcard, a drawing. Sometimes, when I received a letter from her, I noticed that it had already been opened. Other times, she didn't get my letters. She sometimes told me how difficult it was for her to compete and study at the same time. Divided as I'd always been between my sport and school, I understood only too well.

She never talked about money problems, up to the end. Times were truly hard for Russia; at one point, we never knew if the Russians would make it to competitions. When they did come, they had often travelled by train, overnight, and arrived the day of the meet, exhausted.

I would have liked to persuade Gana to come to Montreal, but she had told me this would be almost impossible. A circus artist and a synchronized swimming coach like Gana's parents were not likely to be the most sought-after immigrants, even though they spoke several languages, including French and English. No, even if I complained sometimes, life wasn't necessarily easy for the other competitors.

Synchronized swimming enabled me to travel all over the world: Japan, Egypt, Germany, France, Puerto Rico, Switzerland, Greece, Spain, Fiji, Australia, New Zealand.

Australia and New Zealand . . . but I'm getting ahead of myself. Far, very far from home, there were trips full of laughter with Julie and a group of girls, there was Gana's friendship, and there was Paul, too . . .

FOUR

Prince Charming

Dear Paul. Everything happened so long ago. You had your Olympic thrill, you had your medal. Now, here in Barcelona, it's my turn. Watch me swim!

I hadn't really had any boyfriends up till then. How stupid we felt, Nathalie Audet and I, hearing the other girls talk about their first loves. When confidences were shared in the locker room, we listened and blushed. Then we shrank with fear that the other girls would ask us, "And how about you?"

Some evenings, the girls went out dancing. Despite their repeated invitations, we went home like good girls and listened to records to find new music for our routines. Anyway, I didn't know how to dance, and I looked ridiculous. The few times I let the others drag me out, I sat glued to my chair.

It didn't matter if people thought I was old-fashioned. For me, all that counted were school and synchronized swimming. It was the same for Nathalie. Because we had each other for company, we felt less ridiculous.

But Julie was in despair over my shyness and my inability to express emotion in the water. My movements were very acceptable technically, but everything was mechanical, hard, cold. Looking back, she laughs and says, "If only you'd had a boyfriend like the others, it might have softened you up."

For a short time, I did have a friend, when I was around fourteen. His name was Benoît. Every Friday evening in the winter, he spent two hours on the bus to come and see me at home after training. In the summer, he made the trip by bicycle. The other six days of the week, we talked on the phone.

After a year and a half, tired of the rigorous schedule, he gave me an ultimatum: "It's swimming or me."

For me, there was no choice. I cried my eyes out, and I continued swimming.

I got over my broken heart and swore that I wouldn't let it happen again. So my life was limited to school and training when Cocotine and I went to the Australia games, where I would swim a duet with her in addition to my solo. It was our first competition together. Cocotine was my nickname for Nathalie. In return, she called me Cocotte, while all the other CAMO swimmers called me Karine. Even today, she's my best friend and the only person I know who can eat a dozen muffins one after the other, just like me.

After Nathalie arrived at CAMO, my relationship with Julie changed a little. Nathalie was from Quebec City, and she didn't have the CAMO culture in her heart like I did. For me, Julie was God. I never would have dreamed of arguing with her: I listened and obeyed, period. Nathalie, on the other hand, gave advice, asked questions, sometimes even argued. Gently, without my really noticing, she helped me loosen up a little. Things that were so important to me, things I would never dare say to Julie, Nathalie said for me. Then I began to express myself, too. I was turning from a little girl into an adolescent. It was about time, since I was almost eighteen.

Sometimes, we laughed at Julie's little quirks. A year before, I would have felt like I was committing a sacrilege.

But Nathalie opened my eyes: could it be that Julie was human, after all? Friendship between us, impossible as long as I kept her on her inaccessible pedestal, now blossomed. More than my coach, she became my companion, my confidante — perhaps more vulnerable, but warmer, too.

But, where was I? Oh, yes, Australia. What a trip!

Like all girls our age, we made fun of anyone and everyone. In the cafeteria, there was an employee whose face was a constant source of amusement. Because of his long pointy nose, we called him "Emu," like those ridiculous big birds, the little cousins of ostriches, that are found in Australia. We giggled shamelessly, even when he was around, until, after a few days, he came over and said, in hesitant French, "Hello, I speak a little of your language . . ."

Since just the three of us — Nathalie, Julie, and I — had made the trip, we had gotten closer since we arrived. Our lodgings helped. We were staying in a monastery, in small cells. When I opened my cot the first night, I saw a swarm of things crawling on my mattress: it was infested with insects.

Standing on Nathalie's bed, I laughed, I cried, but mostly I shrieked. The soldiers who were guarding the athletes' village came running with their aerosol cans. Attack!

That night, while Nathalie slept like a log, completely oblivious to every insect on earth, I dozed in a chair at the foot of the bed. In her room, Julie wasn't doing any better than me. A little earlier, she had burst into our room, almost hysterical. She had seen a "hole" on her wall. When the hole started to move, Julie screamed, and the gallant soldiers once again launched an assault against the intruder. "Pow!" Instead of aerosol sprays, it was a well-aimed dustpan that vanquished the large spider taking its nightly stroll in Julie's room. Abracadabra! No more hole . . .

It was on this completely zany note that our visit began. The competition had its absurd moments, too. It had taken us six months to perfect our duet, but right in the middle, Nathalie had a memory lapse. Since my back was to her, I didn't notice that our movements weren't completely coordinated. For long seconds, in utter panic, she simply did whatever came to mind.

The error was so obvious that the judges couldn't believe their eyes. At this level of competition, no one made such mistakes, especially not the Canadians.

At the edge of the pool, utterly distraught but not wanting to let it show too much, Julie had a silly smile on her face. Nathalie was squirming, and I was laughing. It had happened to Nathalie, but it could just as easily have happened to me. And when we saw the marks, there really wasn't too much damage. Although the error had been flagrant, the judges hadn't known what to make of it. They, perhaps, thought it had been an elegant touch of originality. In the end, we came home with two victories, in duet and solo.

But I'm getting ahead of myself, yet again.

Paul and Grant, his best friend, were two New Zealand swimmers. Paul Kingsman was a backstroker, one of the best in his country. He was also a nice, tall blond boy who wouldn't hurt a flea. We had seen him and Grant at the movies, where *Jewels of the Nile* was playing.

At one point, one of the actors said, "Who are you? Where are you?" From the middle of the theatre, Paul answered, "I'm here." We all laughed.

He was Prince Charming to a girl with stars in her eyes. In fact, I wanted my Prince Charming to be good-looking and romantic, of course, but above all, I wanted him to be funny.

Grant had a soft spot for Nathalie. As soon as we had a little free time, we went out on a double date. Paul and I made a rather childish promise: whenever we were separated, we would think of each other at 11:11 every night.

At the end of the meet, Nathalie and I were supposed to spend three days at another swimmer's cottage. Paul and

Grant came to meet us. One night, we all slept around a campfire by the ocean.

But everything must come to an end. Our two handsome swimmers had to leave, for their mothers were waiting for them at the airport. Filled with nostalgia, on the verge of tears, I tried to imagine everything he was doing: "His plane takes off in ten minutes . . . Now he's in the air. That's it, it's over! Oh, Nathalie! We'll never see them again."

We spent several hours on the beach without enjoying it a bit and were about to walk up the road to the cottage when we saw a car driving down the main road, and the people in it were shouting and waving their arms. But who could have recognized us here, in the far reaches of Australia? The car stopped a little farther on, and our two crazy guys got out. They couldn't bring themselves to leave, so Paul had pretended that he was sick. His best friend, who couldn't leave him in the lurch, had gone to the hospital with him. It worked like a charm: the doctors let them go, but those clowns had managed to slip away from the team and their strict coaches — and to miss their plane.

But they still weren't sure that they'd be able to find us. They had come to the cottage at night, without noticing anything but the number of the highway. But, in the end, it wasn't complicated, because the road was straight, almost an expressway. The problem was knowing where to stop. Relying on luck, they hitchhiked. If we hadn't crossed the road at just that moment, we might never have seen them again. The fact that their plan was completely senseless impressed me even more. Now I was sure that Paul loved me!

Our relationship lasted a year and a half. We wrote and called each other while Paul was studying in the United States. And we each kept training. Our long-distance love wasn't very intrusive. From time to time, we'd manage to meet at a competition: "Arrange to get on the team," we'd urge each other. "We'll finally get to see each other . . ."

We saw each other at the Commonwealth Games in Edinburgh in 1986. In spite of the very early curfew, Paul would sometimes sneak out and find me. We would talk, but not for long. He took his sport as seriously as I took mine. In Edinburgh, he won two gold medals, and I won the solo.

The same year, our paths crossed at the World Aquatic Championships in Madrid. While my team and I were winning the gold medal for Canada, he made the final in his specialty. For both of us, there was more than just the competition. We had so much to say to each other. He wanted me to come and live with him in New Zealand.

I saw Paul again at the Seoul Olympic Games in 1988, but on television this time. Because I'd refused to go and train in Calgary, I couldn't participate in the Games. But I don't want to think about such awful things right now. Later . . .

In Seoul, Paul was racing Canadian Mark Tewksbury, his biggest rival. When he won the bronze medal, I cried, oh how I cried.

It was getting more and more difficult for me to see him. Since the world championships, then the Games, he had become a major sports star in his country, and he was very busy. I could understand. It's so demanding sometimes.

When I saw him for the last time, at the 1990 Commonwealth Games in his home country, New Zealand, I was already going out with Sylvain. Paul was at his last competition, and his fiancée was with him. At any rate, by that time he was nothing more than a pleasant memory.

"Tell me Paul," I asked him, "what does Olympic glory feel like? How do you manage to live without the sport?"

It's funny: when it comes right down to it, we didn't know each other that well. My English wasn't very good. And when I think about it, I didn't even know what he was studying. To tell the truth, at that time I was much more in love with my training and school than with anyone in particular.

In a year and a half, that dream had begun and ended.

I was beginning to see several young men, to have little flirtations . . .

François was a lifeguard at the pool. He was the most handsome boy one could imagine, and all the girls had a crush on him. Why did he choose me? No doubt because I was as unsociable as he was. In fact, he suffered from an almost pathological shyness. All the same, at least once, we were able to be daring. François was a dentistry student. I had always wanted to be a doctor. (Nathalie and I had the same dreams: to go to the Olympic Games and be doctors. I ended up going to the Games, and Nathalie ended up being a doctor. It's as if, between us, we managed to accomplish both our dreams.)

As a physical-education student, I was fascinated with muscles and the human body. To satisfy my curiosity, François took me to watch a more "practical" class in which the professor used a cadaver. Far from being disgusted, I found the class simply thrilling. I mixed in with the other students, and no one noticed me. At that time, I wasn't well known.

I had an adolescent crush on François. I waited for him every evening . . . just in case. Instead of having supper when I got home from the pool, I made myself beautiful for him. And then, I waited. But nothing was more important to him than his studies. For six months I felt like I was doing nothing but waiting. This delirium began to interfere with my performance.

It was Karine who brought me back to my senses: "Wake up, girl! You're more attached than he is to this relationship; his studies are taking more and more time. Are you going to let yourself go like this? It's time for it to end."

Karine was right. When I broke it off, I felt like I was cutting into my flesh. As usual, I cried my eyes out, then I plunged back into my sport.

François remained a friend, and it was much better that way. Even when I was living with Sylvain, he continued to write me funny, slightly loony letters. From time to time, I still get a letter addressed to my cats . . .

There were others: Gilles was a neighbouring cottager and a wonderful dancer. Even though she was older than me, his sister Viviane was my best friend in the country. As we sat by the fire, she read me my horoscope, predicting that I'd be very happy, while Gilles played his guitar.

One day, a bunch of us decided to go for a hike in the nearby mountains, as we had done many times. Viviane and I walked on ahead, gossiping. We were getting ready to climb a hill when we saw something move. It was alive, without a doubt. Some kind of animal, obviously, but what kind? Carefully, wordlessly, we went back to the group.

It was the others who noticed the traces. "Look, bear tracks, and they're still fresh." We decided to play fearless woodsmen, or something. I don't really know why, but we all, the entire Potvin family and I, began to follow the trail that led into the woods. Suddenly, we came face-to-face with two baby bears, who looked at us curiously, and their mom, who had just returned to them.

Eight-year-old Stéphane, the Potvins' nephew, wasn't intimidated at all: "I want to touch the big bear."

"Come on, boy, run!"

That day, I think I broke Ben Johnson's record!

Then there was Frédéric, a city boy. Every morning, we met in the bus. He was a university student, like me, but it was only later that I found out he was studying law. We didn't talk at the time. Frédéric wasn't particularly handsome, but his face glowed with some sort of pride. One morning, when I got on the bus, he was reading an article in *La Presse* about me, which was accompanied by a photo. He looked at the photo, surprised, then looked at me. Back and forth, again and again, until we both began to laugh.

Now, every day, when we got on the bus, we felt like we were on a date. We still didn't talk much. Once, he came over to do a crossword puzzle with me, and things went on from there. One day a crossword, the next a hockey game on TV. Together, we ate lobster for the first time. We didn't know exactly what to do, and we both looked a little ridiculous. So we laughed, clumsy but happy together. He had a little red Subaru, a real jalopy, and ugly to boot, but it still took us on a trip around the Gaspé peninsula.

Until then, my first meeting with my lovers had always been gentle, reassuring times, not like Sylvain. With Sylvain everything was so different, so intense . . .

FIVE

Ouch!

Good, it's finally over! But what's happening? I feel so empty. Will I be able to get to the edge of the pool? Dear God, give me strength . . .

I've always had a tendency to overdo things. I was the first to arrive at the pool, and the last to leave. This Olympic-style routine was pure folly, at the limits of human endurance. But the feeling of always going a little farther, almost too far, has always excited me.

I had left adolescence behind and been an integral part of the Canadian team for some time when I received a note from a Canadian judge. At every competition, the judges sent participants a note with their remarks, criticisms, and suggestions. That year, I was wearing a yellow swimsuit with two black stripes on each side to make me look a little slimmer. I must admit, I did have a little extra flesh there.

The note had none of the usual comments; just two messages: the score, as usual, and these four words: "To the yellow elephant." How I cried. In my diary, I usually started my account of the day by drawing a "happy face." That day, there was no happy face, and no smile. That day, I think I even forgot my diary entirely. Then, when I'd finished snivelling, I gritted my teeth.

So, I'm too fat, Madam Judge? All right, you'll see my ribs soon, I promise.

I began to train like a maniac. If I couldn't possibly keep going, I did anyway. If I was tired, worn out, sick to my stomach, all the better; it proved that I'd worked, that I'd pushed myself. Go ahead, fatso, you'll lose your blubber.

But training alone wasn't enough, and I knew it. The best way to get thin, of course, was to stop eating. When my mother urged me to have my dinner, I said that I had just eaten. I had no more than a mouthful of whatever was on my plate; an apple and a Diet Coke were enough, after all. And to quiet the grumbling in my stomach, from time to time I ate half a muffin. I counted my calories carefully, to know how many more I had to burn in training.

I was visibly melting away. Oh, yes, you could see my ribs. In fact, after a little while, you could see them easily, along with my hip bones and my vertebrae.

Julie, who knew me better than I knew myself, was not completely fooled. "My girl, perhaps a swimmer who's too fat doesn't look great, but neither does one who's too thin. And I ask so much of you in training, you need the strength. By not eating, you're beginning to consume your muscles. You don't even float anymore."

So, she forced me to go and weigh myself. "At 1.77 metres, you shouldn't weigh less than sixty-four kilograms. If you drop below that, you won't be strong enough to train anymore. It would be dangerous."

I did weigh myself. But since Julie didn't insist on accompanying me to the scale, I added a few kilograms when I reported back to her, and she continued to coach me.

Nothing seemed to make me see reason, except extreme measures. It was synchronized swimming itself that finally knocked some sense into me. At the 1991 World Cup, in

Bonn, I placed fifth in compulsory figures. Unable to float because my fat level was much too low, I sank when I did each figure, and I just managed to eke out a victory. Whether this alone would have been enough to convince me, I don't know, for there was something else, too.

Julie had filmed me, as she sometimes did. A film is a souvenir, of course, but it also makes it easier to catch errors. Watching it, I suddenly saw a girl I didn't know.

"Who's that?" I asked.

It was me. I had changed so much that I didn't recognize myself. Now, I understood. It was my own fault I had almost lost, and repentant, I was ready to do anything to make up for it, even eat.

This craziness could have cost me dearly. Indeed, although my brain registered the message, my stomach rebelled. Used to having to digest only morsels, it didn't want to be full. It was in Puerto Rico, during the training camp preceding the Olympics, that this precious organ made its wishes known.

To learn how to cope with the heat in Barcelona, we had chosen Puerto Rico as our training site. But the heat and the pre-Olympic stress melted away the weight I had put back on.

Convinced that I was dieting again, Julie decided to lay down the law, once and for all. "Go back to your room," she told me. "You aren't training today. I don't want to have an accident on my conscience. When you've gained a little more weight, you'll come back, but not before!"

Not train anymore, so close to the Olympics? It wasn't possible. How could Julie do this to me?

After half a day away from the pool, and feeling awful because I'd missed my morning training session, I tried to explain things to her. She should have done this to me last year, not now, because I *was* eating normally. In fact, I was eating even more than normal, but I simply couldn't gain any weight.

We were at our wits' end when we thought of the weightlifters, who were also in Puerto Rico to get acclimatized before the Games. When it came to food, they were total pigs, and they would be terribly offended if someone sat with them gnawing on an apple or a celery stalk. They were the ideal dinner companions for a girl looking to put on a few kilos.

Finally, by eating five meals a day, I managed to gain a little weight. I never did get to sixty-six kilos, which would have been my ideal weight, but I did reach sixty-five, which wasn't too bad. And finally we could breathe a little easier.

I had known weightlifters when I was doing bodybuilding. How I had hated weight training at first! The idea had come from American Tracy Ruiz, Olympic champion in 1984, who had married a bodybuilder. When she made her comeback in 1987, we didn't recognize her. Just an ordinary girl in 1984, three years later she had a superb body, with sharply defined muscles. She was both beautiful and athletic, and we were all full of wide-eyed admiration. Especially me, who had never really liked her artistic style and had envied her charisma. To see her like this, swimming her guts out, gave me goose bumps.

Julie wanted us to be more powerful and more defined as well, so she decided that we would do some bodybuilding, too. She found the ideal man to be our trainer: Andrzej Kulesza, who eventually became just André to us. He had been a national weightlifting coach, but he was also a physiologist, and he put together a program adapted to women and to swimmers.

Nathalie Guay, my duet partner at the time, and I had to serve as guinea pigs. It was so horrible that it would have been hard to choose between weightlifting and a medieval torture chamber! André tried everything he could to encourage us, both firmness and kindness, but nothing worked; instead, we listened to our poor, aching muscles. Although we were exhausted, we had enough energy left to express our rage. André had told us, "You should put down the weights gently, never throw them." From time to time — quite often, to tell the truth — frustration led us to ignore his wise advice. Bang! That's what we think of your bodybuilding, Mr. Kulesza! And where are the results you promised? You've been making us sweat for months!

Finally, after a year of these gruelling sessions, we began to see the results — and feel them, too. "Tell me, André," I asked, "is this little bump a muscle?" For me, who had been about as muscular as a kitten, it was a true miracle. "Hey, Natou, it works!"

This discovery amounted to a revelation, a thunderbolt. I began to lift weights like never before. If I was happy, I lifted; if I was discouraged, I lifted; if I was frustrated, I lifted . . . just five kilos more.

André was as happy with my new enthusiasm as a missionary is with a conversion, and he sometimes did me the honour of a little private competition. Gradually, he became my training partner. He lifted and pressed much more weight than I did, of course, but I sometimes managed to raise my mark by a kilo or two while he had to content himself with the same weight as the last time. It was ridiculous, but I got a sort of pride, a childish pleasure, from it.

One time, I beat him at an exercise, managing thirty repetitions to his twenty-seven. "The thrill of victory," as they would say on *The Wide World of Sports*! A new medal couldn't have made me happier.

As I trained, I reached heights I had thought inaccessible: fifteen repetitions with an eighty-kilo weight in the squat, three repetitions with sixty-two-and-a-half kilos in the bench press. My fat ratio fell to eleven percent.

My new enthusiasm, however, had no effect on the others. In spite of the solid muscles that were forming under their skin, Nathalie, and then the Vilagos twins, who joined me in the torture chamber when they returned to competition, remained cool to the "joys" of muscle building.

Our coach was thrilled. Not only were our bodies more athletic and beautiful, but they were more symmetrical. The weaker leg that had always made us lean to one side no longer got in the way. Along with our appearance, our movements were edging toward perfection. And we had more power: with my stronger back muscles, I could get even higher out of the water than ever before.

Although the bodybuilding experiment did yield positive results, our experiences as guinea pigs were not always as happy. Just ask the Vilagos twins what they thought of nasal prostheses.

"If only you didn't have to wear those horrible nose plugs," people said sometimes. Obviously, we felt the same way.

In fact, a Dutch swimmer had recently started wearing a nasal prosthesis that was completely invisible. She came to train at CAMO for a while, and we, like St. Thomas, were able to see the apparatus for ourselves. She put it in and took it out as if it were no more complicated than wearing earplugs.

We wanted to have the same thing. We started to work on it after the Canadian championships, but we had to keep our plans secret until the Olympic Games so that it would be a surprise. We found a specialist to make the mould and then the nasal prostheses. He was an orthodontist, who was used to working with such things . . . except that noses and teeth aren't exactly the same. Not wanting to experiment on us, he first inflicted the procedure he had thought up on himself. And he didn't even need a prosthesis! The poor man injected the silicone so deeply that he had to go to the hospital.

At least, the experience was useful. That way, he knew just what what to do when it came to our turn.

Bodybuilding was nothing compared to this. The first time, the silicone was too liquid and spread a little too far. I had a truly depilatory experience getting it out; a little farther and I would have pulled out my brain. The makers of hair-removal wax should think about it: there's nothing like a mixture of Vaseline and silicone — it will yank out everything it comes into contact with.

Another time, the silicone wasn't liquid enough and enlarged my nostrils so much that I looked like a grotesque cow. I'm sure we all would have laughed if we hadn't had such sore noses and been so discouraged. Every time he worked on us, the orthodontist, aware of the pain he was inflicting since he had already experienced it himself, gave us a despairing look and apologized. Because he was very nice, we didn't complain too much, but we would blow our noses for three hours after we left his office.

The little apparatus that was causing us such trouble was working like a charm for the Dutch girl. Apparently, her nose was completely straight, almost devoid of cartilage; still, there had to be a way to make it work, even for us . . .

We didn't give up. Finally, we got our prostheses. But they had to go deep into our nostrils and weren't at all comfortable. Inserting and removing them was torture. The most nerve-wracking thing was that they tickled constantly and made us sneeze throughout our training sessions.

Just before the Olympics, we admitted defeat. Not because of the pain and the sneezing, but because fear had replaced our determination: we didn't know if the prostheses were really waterproof. A single drop of water in the nostrils burned horribly. The Games were already stressful enough, and we had no desire to be even more anxious because of the prostheses. We would be a little less beautiful, and that was that!

Some people say that all elite athletes are a little masochistic. That may be true, because we know better than anyone else that we have to suffer to succeed, to surpass our limits . . . Everyone has her own Karine inside to remind her of this.

Tendonitis and bursitis are part of daily life. We tell ourselves, "You're not going to stop swimming just because you have a pulled muscle. Bandage it up tight and off you go."

We never give in to self-pity: "So you broke up with your boyfriend? Do your crying after training . . ."

But the worst part is the minor injuries, the little aches and pains and illnesses that affect everyone but that an athlete must ignore.

It was the autumn of 1990, and the 1991 world championships were just a month and a half away. One morning, I had a shock when I got up. My cheek was so swollen that my whole face was distorted. My eye was just a slit.

"We'll have to pull your wisdom teeth," the dentist told me. "If you like, I can do just one side, but it's very possible you won't want me to continue after that . . ."

Why wouldn't I want him to continue? What a funny idea. Since I didn't ask why, the dentist didn't explain, knowing that I would find out what he meant soon enough.

Oh, I knew it would be painful, obviously. But I was a hardened athlete, I had been in pain before . . .

"Pull them all out!" I told him.

As fascinated as ever with anything to do with medicine, I asked for mirrors so that I could watch everything. I was proud of myself, for I behaved in a very dignified manner.

I was driving home when the anaesthetic began to wear off. I stopped at my grandmother's. Though she tried to pretend that nothing was out of the ordinary, my cousin Mélanie couldn't help staring at me. The expression on her face couldn't have been more revealing: I looked like a monster.

My composure, which I'd been so proud of in the dentist's office, melted away with one look at my face. "Please, Grandpa," I pleaded, "drive me home."

Lying on my bed, I cried while Mom stroked my hair and

told me all kinds of stories. I didn't say a word. In fact, I couldn't even open my mouth.

I remembered that Mom had been through this herself. Insensitive as only a child could be, I had invited my friends to see the show: "Come see my mother. She looks like she has a grapefruit in each cheek. She's so ugly, she looks like a monster." Now, I was the one with the grapefruits.

The next day, I was supposed to take part in a photo session at the University of Montreal to immortalize the principal muscles of the human body for an anatomy text-book for phys-ed students. For the occasion, they had gathered several specimens of muscular development, among them speed skater Nathalie Lambert and weightlifter Alain Bilodeau.

As soon as he saw my sorry condition, the professor let me leave. "Go home to bed," he told me.

But there was also my training: "Julie, I can't train today."

"All right for this once," she said. "But I want to see you back in the pool Monday."

I panicked. The championships were just around the corner, and things were going from bad to worse. I couldn't eat anything but yogurt and Jell-O. My steak and potatoes had to be put through the blender. As for my appearance, it was better not to think about it. My mother had looked like a monster, but she got back to normal after a while. On the other hand, I looked more like the Elephant Man every day.

The dentist at the emergency clinic pronounced his verdict: "Your mouth is full of thrush." That this was a kind of viral ulcer didn't interest me at all. All I knew was that it hurt like the devil.

Finally, as casually as he could, the dentist added, "Could you go to the University of Montreal laboratory? I'd like to take photos of this, I've never seen anything so disgusting."

"Mr. Dentist, sir, this is my mouth you're talking about!" I retorted.

A few days later, I went to Calgary anyway to have my routine evaluated by Canadian judges. When they saw me, they were nonplussed. I couldn't even smile. I could swim with torn muscles and make it look like I was in perfect shape, but this I couldn't hide. In spite of everything, they took pity on me and gave me a passing mark!

All my life I've been prone to infections because of my low white-blood-cell count. When I was a little girl, my doctor even thought that I had leukemia. He conducted various tests, including the horrible bone-marrow extraction. It wasn't leukemia or diabetes, but my white-blood-cell count was still abnormally low. Most people have between six and twelve thousand, but I had just two thousand; at a count of seventeen or eighteen hundred, a person is hospitalized.

The doctor explained it to me this way: "The white blood cells are like little soldiers in your blood. They fight infections and illnesses. You don't have lots of little soldiers, but they fight very hard." In spite of my little soldiers' valour, I was more vulnerable to infections. I didn't get colds, like everyone else, but bronchitis.

We all shaved our legs and bikini lines before competitions. One time, we decided to wax them instead.

After some time, a pimple formed on my groin and started to grow. A hair had grown into the skin, causing an infection. The pimple soon grew into an enormous, black, disgusting lump.

The doctor was categorical: "We have to lance it. But with the sutures, it'll be two weeks before you can go in the water again."

Two weeks! It was completely out of the question. We were leaving for Japan the next day, and I had to swim the solo for Canada.

Finally, we compromised. He would lance it, since he had to, but he would then apply a very tight dressing and leave the incision to heal naturally. The infection was much deeper than he had thought. Nevertheless, he kept his word.

I swam in the competition, and I even won. In the water, the slight blood-tinged discharge was invisible. When I got out of the pool, I sponged away the repugnant liquid, without looking, and held the dressing tight until the next time I went in.

I could no longer do without my sport. It was my passion, my drug. I think they would have to cut off both my legs to keep me from swimming.

Take my hip, for example. Since I was very young, I've always been able to bend myself into a pretzel. Literally. The splits have always been easy for me to do, even with my head in the water, when gravity couldn't help me gain a few extra centimetres. On land, I could do the splits with one leg on the ground and the other on a chair. In the water, I have always been one of the few competitors who could do a 180-degree split, which has always impressed people. But not me. What impressed me was the results of work. The splits were natural, there was nothing impressive about them.

I could dislocate all my joints. Although this extreme flexibility was an asset in competition, there were times in daily life when my freedom of movement cost me dearly.

"Run yourself a nice hot bath, my girl, and I'll make you a nice omelet," Mom said one evening, interrupting her phone conversation.

I had just swum in the preliminaries, and I was to swim in the finals the next day. That evening, I felt like I'd been run over by a steamroller; my kidneys, in particular, were killing me. A hot bath would be very soothing. As I leaned over the bathtub, my body seized up. Completely. The doctors would say it was a sacroiliac sprain, but I knew that my hip had come out of its socket.

"Mom! Mom!"

Still on the phone, Mom heard me with one ear but kept talking.

Miserable and in agony, I dragged myself to her bed. That's where she found me, trembling, my hip completely dislocated.

Martin went out with a garbage bag and filled it with snow to put on my hip. Then Mom called the chiropractor. He wasn't surprised; after all, it wasn't the first time he'd come to put a joint back in place.

"It would be better if you don't swim," he told me. "That would be the wise thing to do."

"If I can swim, I will."

This was neither stubbornness nor courage. I had no choice. It was the day before a competition, and I was a member of the team. I couldn't let the other seven girls down. The team is sacred, and all swimmers know that. Eight girls train together for months, so there's no question of anyone leaving the others in the lurch at the last minute for the least little thing.

As well, it would have been impossible to find a replacement, for the team had always needed my strength. When a girl had to be lifted out of the water, I was the one to do it. "Now smile!" I'd whisper. "And don't worry, I'm holding you!" In my duet with Nathalie Guay, we had created a new move: I threw her out of the water and caught her by an ankle. The number of times we missed before mastering this move was incredible. Yet how we loved it when we got it! But I'm getting away from the subject.

There was a competition coming up, and I had to do the boosts — no one could replace me. So I had to swim. But when I dove into the pool for training, pow! My hip dislocated again.

"Julie! Julie!"

The chiropractor treated me all day. Even if I couldn't

do my solo, I'd be there for the team in the competition. I simply warned the girls: "If I yell, come."

They all swam the routine with their heads slightly turned toward me. But no one had to come running.

In the water, I've always felt invulnerable. It's as if, in my special world, everything is possible. In fact, I feel less sure of myself, less safe, on dry land. The worst moment was when I had a car accident. A van coming in the opposite direction crashed into my car. When I got out, I was slightly hurt: the keys and dashboard buttons had imprinted themselves on my knees, and my neck and back hurt. I was crying, of course, as I always did, but there was no serious injury. The guy who had hit me was in worse shape. He came out of it unscathed, too, except that he didn't have a driver's permit. This accident was likely to be very expensive for him.

It was only when I turned around to look at my car that I realized what had happened. The body was completely demolished. Oh, my God! This is how one dies in a car accident. Is this how my father died?

It was an all-black Laser, like the one Sylvain used . . . Why does everything come back to that?

There's just one more thing I want to talk about, even though it's a bit of a taboo among swimmers. In general, athletes are afraid of injuries, illness, anything that could keep them from competing. Synchronized swimmers have one fear that grips them even more than their fear of the judges or cold water: suffocating underwater from holding our breath too long. To get rid of this fear, to try to master it, they even organize group-therapy sessions.

I once told a journalist that when I was small, I was unable to stay underwater for more than thirteen seconds. He thought that was my lifetime record and reported it that way. I hope he never tries holding his breath underwater for that long, for he wouldn't have time to see much! In fact, a well-trained swimmer can stay underwater for about forty-five seconds during a very difficult figure, a minute and a half in the compulsories, and almost three minutes without moving. But this doesn't happen all by itself.

When we were very small, we were scared of suffocating, and our heads popped out of the water well before our lungs gave us the signal. Julie would time us, and none of us could go beyond twenty seconds. During underwater hockey games, though, we easily went beyond forty seconds, because we didn't think about it when we were busy playing.

We have all felt this fear in the pit of our stomachs. Yet what impresses the judges, aside from difficulty, is the ability to perform movements and routines without coming up for air. Certain exercises are actually evaluated according to these two combined elements: perfection of execution and time spent with the head underwater.

In compulsories, both the desire to win and fear can sometimes push us into costly errors. In the compulsory figures, the movements must be performed as slowly and smoothly as possible to demonstrate maximum control. What counts above all is to attain the right balance. If we want to impress the judges so much that we go too slowly, we have to speed up at the end so we don't suffocate, and the rhythm is broken. Points off! If fear takes over and we don't want to take the risk, we'll probably hurry our movements and come back to the surface too soon, while our lungs still contain quite a bit of air. The quality of the performance is thus considerably reduced, and so is the mark.

The idea is to push oneself to the limit of one's abilities. But how do we go very far without going *too* far? How can I know when it's time to listen to Sylvie, who's suffocating, and send Karine, who's urging me on, away?

As I approach my limit, I feel like someone is turning the lights on and off. That's the signal: I know that I have just a few more seconds, maybe less, and I want to use them to my advantage: it might make all the difference. It doesn't hurt. On the contrary, I feel euphoric and think that perhaps this time I'm not hyperventilating, as this problem is called. Lights on, lights off, lights on, lights off. Suddenly, without warning, the lights go off and don't come on again.

Sometimes the swimmer sinks, but usually her movements become uncoordinated and her eyes go blank. And then Julie jumps in, if one of the girls hasn't already gone to her teammate's rescue.

And afterwards, it's painful! It causes a terrible headache, sometimes accompanied by muscle spasms that make the legs jerk.

Then, for a while, we are all a bit more careful . . .

SIX

The Ups and Downs of a Synchronized Swimmer

So, you want to squeeze out those extra points? Look, my feet are all blue, as usual. What would all those people say, if they saw them? Do Olympic feet really look like that?

If competition brought only tendonitis and all the other horrible "itises" that one can imagine, from swimmer's otitis (ear inflammation) to the arthritis that lies in wait for our ageing bones when we're in our thirties, we would have to be totally crazy or completely stunned to get involved. But there's more, much more.

I was only eleven when I took part in my first Canadian championships. By then, I had been "married" for some time to an older girl for the duet. Suzanne Grenier, who was stronger than me, wasn't too thrilled with the big "baby" who had fallen into her arms, so I did my utmost to keep up with her. I never complained; on the contrary, all I asked was always to stretch myself a little farther.

So I went into this first championship with Suzanne. Since the beginning, there was one part of our routine that always caused us problems. No matter what we did, we couldn't manage to count it in the same way, and the synchronization fell apart. Julie, never at her wits' end, thought up a solution: "Macaroni! Say 'macaroni' and move your head on each syllable."

In the end, we were ranked twenty-third out of twenty-four. In spite of all my efforts to rise to the occasion, I lagged behind, and our duet really wasn't balanced. Still, the pride I felt performing my few little arm movements was incredible. Two years later, I won the Canadian junior championship in solo and duet — quite an accomplishment, considering that the junior category was for swimmers fifteen years and under.

My style at the time was, to say the least, unemotional. To tell the truth, it hadn't changed much since I started. As long as I kept my head underwater, there was no problem: I did figures well, I was strong and flexible, a true champion. But everything fell apart when my head came back to the surface and I had to do something with my long arms.

"Pretend you're stroking your doll," Julie told me.

I never had many dolls and didn't really know what to do with them. And so I felt completely ridiculous. All the other girls — Natou, Annie — made cute, even elegant, little gestures; why not me? I was the best in compulsories, but, unfortunately, the worst in solo.

"Pretend you're carrying crystal glasses," Julie told me.

If I had really been carrying them, they would have shattered into a thousand pieces long ago. With me, nothing worked.

Julie was almost ready to give up on making me into a solo swimmer, a discipline that requires more softness and emotion. I couldn't even smile. In desperation, she created the "Sylvie Fréchette" style — a jerky, rhythmic, quasi-military style that was perfect for a frigid swimmer. I looked like a soldier — a soldier! — and no one else's music sounded anything like mine.

I consoled myself by telling myself that I was stronger in the "egg-beater," the leg-rotation movement, so that I rose higher and maintained my position longer than the others. Technically, perhaps, I was champion material. But on the artistic side, we'd have to think again.

I was well aware of my physical strength. So were all the kids in the neighbourhood. I was a good thirty centimetres taller than them, and after my victories in arm wrestling they called me "king" of the alley. I was thirteen. I may have been strong, but I sure wasn't artistic! I would have to reveal some other facet of my personality and, perhaps, my weaknesses.

I swam my solos, which were supposed to be softer, as if they were duets, with the more abrupt movements I would make if I were synchronizing with an imaginary partner.

For me, hell could be summed up in one short sentence from Julie: "Stand in front of the mirror and create an arm." Create an arm! I would rather have cut it off! Inevitably, I turned red with shame and was incapable of finding the slightest inspiration.

In 1986, when I was a solid second in Canada and a member of the national team, Natou and Martine Labelle had to create the arm movements that I would use to accompany my Elton John music, since I couldn't do it. And again, my execution was only a pale imitation of what they could do. Those few movements at the beginning, before I jumped into the water, were the worst part. One would have sworn that I was a fish out of water.

Not only was I awkward at creating arm movements, I was also embarrassed when it was time to buy my clothes. Even now, my mother helps me choose my swimsuits, as she once chose my entire wardrobe. I still find it hard to buy clothes without her approval. When I started swimming, she was as inexperienced at buying swimsuits as I was; the ones she chose were ones she could have worn. One of them was completely straight across the bottom, from the crotch and around the hips: a real granny swimsuit. The rules regarding swimsuits have always been very specific: legs cut to the waist are not allowed; the suit must come two inches below the hip bone, so that it is well covered. And watch out — they measure! But swimsuits more modest than that wouldn't do.

So I wore an orange one, with bra cups, that Julie lent me. Just because I was tall, didn't mean I couldn't look a bit womanly. The cups were well formed, but I didn't have much to put in them — they were designed to hold real breasts. Not knowing what to do with this new chest, I tried to hide it a bit by pushing the cups in, but all I managed to do was leave deep finger-shaped indents, which made me look worse and didn't help my problem.

My first solo was based on a duet that the girls performed to the music from *Superman*. One couldn't imagine anything more robotic than that.

My music always had a strong, hard beat that matched my movements: "Battlestar Galactica," "Flashdance," and so on. I knew that people were laughing at me a little, but I didn't know how much until some wise guy had the bright idea of inventing video. So now I could see myself: shoulders stuck to my ears, stony face, mechanical arms . . . and if, by chance, I attempted a slightly artistic hand movement, my pointing index finger always transformed it into a vulgar gesture.

Put your head in the water, my girl, and quick!

In spite of this, my family was always there to cheer me on. There must have been fifteen or twenty of them in the stands at the junior championships in Ottawa, yelling, whistling — a band of adorable, noisy, nutty people. And they weren't there just for me: they cheered just as loudly for a young cousin doing his best in a peewee tournament.

As the trophies and medals piled up, my family's enthusiasm for my victories sometimes impinged a little on their tact. "Yes, Sylvie's doing very well," my mother would answer when someone called. "That's right, she's leaving tomorrow . . . It's for such and such a championship . . . Oh, yes, she's in great shape." Then, completely deadpan, she would add, before hanging up, "Yes, and Martin's doing very well, too . . ."

Martin didn't say anything, but he knew. Yes, his big sister sometimes took up a lot of room.

Sometimes, without being too obvious, he would let us know what he thought of the situation. When a swimmer friend called me, Martin said, "That's right, call her Karine. But to us, she's still Sylvie." As far as he was concerned, I was always just his sister, and it was fine that way.

In spite of my rather unorthodox style, I was winning. My victory at the Canadian championships had even opened the door to an international competition in Calgary. To me, it was the top of the world. Besides, although I was competing in the fifteen-and-under solo and duet, the national team, the real one, the one for the "big girls," would also be there for the pan-Pacific championships. Wow! Me and them at the same international competition . . .

Julie wanted to show us the world, as usual, and had driven to Banff in the family car. It was a bumpy trip. We smaller girls were in the back; I sat with my knees squished up against my forehead and slowly turned green. But we loved Lake Louise, with its luxury hotel, and I brought back two sweaters, one for Mom and one for Martin.

The group, the team, was always something special. If one of us looked like she was about to falter, the one that felt the freshest would give the others a bit of encouragement that was imperceptible to anyone but us. It meant, "We're suffering, too, but you can do it. Let's go, we're almost done."

On the other hand, working in a team could also be a little frustrating: for instance, if one of us had to be late for practice because she had something important to do. What could be more important than training?

I always found true partnership in the duets.

I was twelve or thirteen when a new partner was chosen for me: Catherine Paradis, who became Annie. Annie came from a very small club, Bain Lévesque, but she had lots of potential. However, she wasn't used to competing. In one of our first performances, the underwater speaker began to fade out and the music became intermittent. At CAMO, we all knew the rule: If the music stops, you keep going. We had forgotten to tell Annie. Right in the middle of our routine, right in front of the judges, she lifted her head out of the water and yelled: "Julie, we can't hear the music anymore."

We finished last.

Together, we won the Canadian junior championships, then came in third at the pan-Pacific championships in Calgary. We spent entire days trying to find music, fabric, swimsuits. And when we finally found something, we always agreed. We were together for two years.

Then, after being without a partner for a year, I was paired with Chantal Laviolette, at the time a member of the national team. She was nineteen and I was fifteen, so she pushed me really hard. She has since recycled her swimming talent by becoming a coach. When she took over the Neptunettes in Ottawa, she changed everything: their name, style, tracksuits, routines — everything. The club is now emerging as a rising force in Canada, and I see her hand clearly in this.

From time to time, as a change from swimming, I would invite Manon Morin, my neighbour from the other side of the alley, to come over. She was small, and exactly my opposite. We were like Mutt and Jeff. I had started in synchronized swimming with her, and her father used to drive us home from the pool in the evening. As we turned on to 16th Avenue, he would keep hitting the brakes to shake us up: a tap on the gas pedal, then the brakes. It felt like a carnival ride, and we laughed like crazy, especially me, who had always thought of fathers as very serious people. Manon introduced me to hot-dog chips, which I never saw again after that. And we would sneak off together in the evening and make prank phone calls.

Fortunately, by the time we were teenagers, my friends and I had passed this stage of juvenile humour. When we were fifteen or sixteen, our overriding passion was horror movies. On Friday evenings, Catherine Vilcek and I would have our fill. Like Manon, who had quit synchronized swimming long before, Catherine was my window to "something else." Settled in front of Mom's VCR, all we wanted was to be scared. When it was time for her to go home, we always went through the same routine: Catherine, who lived only two doors down from me but was frightened of going that distance in the dark, would make me promise to watch her from my balcony until she reached her door. I would promise, then, slowly, I would count down: "One, two, three, go!" And Catherine would run to her place as fast as she could.

It was during this time when we were taking such pleasure in scaring ourselves that I discovered the difference between a little shiver in front of the TV and true fear. My picture had just appeared in the centrefold of the *Journal de Montréal*. It was the first time that such a large photo of me had appeared anywhere. It wasn't a pinup, but I was in a swimsuit, of course. I was presented as a hopeful, a young girl from Rosemont who was making progress in synchronized swimming . . .

A few jokers found my telephone number in the phone book and called me. Some were sicker than others, saying things like, "If you don't stop, I'll rape you . . ."

One was particularly scary. While the calls were just a passing game for the others, he was persistent: "Is it really you, the swimmer? You know, you're not half bad looking."

It went on for months: "You didn't notice me, but I was right beside you on the bus. You had your Walkman on."

He knew everything — what street I got off at, where I had gone. Now, when the telephone rang, Martin answered, trying to play the "man of the house" with his breaking adolescent voice. Grandpa came to get me at the bus stop with the dog and a crowbar.

I suppose it was a little foretaste of the darker side of fame. In fact, aside from this photo and a short article from time to time, my career was following its steady path in a state of almost complete anonymity.

Nathalie Audet, from Quebec City, was my next partner, and we clicked right away. We were two "good girls" on the same wavelength, and we protected each other from the rest of the world. In the water, this cooperation was enhanced, becoming almost telepathic. We could literally feel what the other felt. She was the only one who always called me Sylvie, no doubt because she came from elsewhere and didn't know about Karine.

My mother became Nathalie's second mother, for her family was back in Quebec City. When I was small, all my friends envied me my mother because she took part in our games or invented new ones for us, she always allowed another friend in, and she almost never said no . . . They didn't seem to notice that I didn't have a father. Nathalie, too, fell under Mom's spell.

Both Nathalie and I had been on the Canadian team since 1983. Our goal was to represent Canada in duet at the world championships in Madrid. But when we came in second at the Canadian championships, we realized that the dream was over. Only the Canadian champion competes at the world championships.

It wasn't losing that was the hardest thing to bear. Our routine was superb. We had come up with a movement that was tiring but very impressive: with one arm in the air, I lifted

Nathalie up with the other outstretched arm. As always, at least I had this profound conviction that we had done our best, which comforted and satisfied me.

No, what was hardest to bear was Nathalie's terrible sadness. Nathalie, who was already talking about retiring, felt the same frustration I felt, but much more deeply. For her, coming in second was the end . . . or almost, since we would be in Madrid with the rest of the team anyway. With the six other girls who formed the Canadian team, we could at least have the small consolation of trying for the gold medal in the world championships. But it was from the stands that we watched the performance of the Canadian duet favoured to win the gold medal.

When Carolyn Waldo and Michelle Cameron jumped into the water, we prayed for them; we held hands, squeezing very hard. Behind our sunglasses, the tears were flowing. Never again would we swim together . . .

Nathalie fulfilled one of our common dreams and became a doctor. I realized the other by taking part in the Olympics. But before I got to that point, there was still a long way to go.

From time to time, I had to get away from it all. Then I went back to my own private world: the cottage. Even today, I can't believe that Grandpa died there, where I was always so happy. And it was there, in 1982, that we celebrated my grandparents' fortieth wedding anniversary. All seven of their children were there with their own broods, so the party was lively, to say the least. That night, everyone slept at the cottage, some stretched out on the floor in the living room, others in tents pitched in the yard. It wouldn't have surprised me to find some hanging from the ceiling.

When I was eighteen or nineteen, I would sometimes get away to the cottage with my brother for a weekend or an entire week at the end of the summer.

"Coming out for a ride?" he would ask.

Knowing very well that Julie would have strangled both of us if she knew, he would bounce me over roots, driving the three-wheeled all-terrain vehicle with me sitting on the metal bar behind him. I came back from our expeditions with my neck like jelly and my coccyx more black than blue, but with a smile on my lips and feeling as happy as a schoolgirl who'd played hooky.

A few times, Martin asked me to take a picture of him doing a wheelie. But when the ATV came toward me, bucking like a wild bronco, I panicked. The photos showed only a bit of wheel, a handlebar, or a speck of dust. And Martin teased me gently: "Scaredy-cat!"

One day, Martin said, "You have strong legs. I bet you'd do okay waterskiing."

He was wrong. My legs were strong, but they were too flexible. I looked like Goofy on skis. And Martin laughed his head off. Waterskiing! If Julie had found out, she would have scalped me: synchronized swimming was a serious business now. At the international level, there was no more fooling around . . .

Nathalie Guay, Natou for short, was my last duet partner, and the one I swam with for the longest time. In our four years together, we learned an incredible amount. If my partnership with Nathalie Audet stemmed from our physical similarities, my partnership with Natou was a triumph over our differences. I was classical, and she was completely zany. Overflowing with imagination, she abandoned herself to her artistic whims. One of our routines, surely among the most beautiful of my career, was punctuated with a telephone ringing — something unheard of.

Nathalie was a bit lazy — just a bit! — but she had amazing talent, which could make anyone die of jealousy, though she never seemed to be really aware of it. Like the other Nathalie, she was smaller than me, but her long limbs reduced the difference considerably. In fact, her small size had its advantages. With the strength of my sixty-eight kilos, I was able to lift her forty-five kilos to incredible heights with ease.

We constantly came up with new things, and we were disappointed when our crazy ideas didn't come to pass. Our partnership was so close that we could swim without music.

The only duet that is a painful memory, the one that hurts the most, is the one I never had.

SEVEN

Crosses to Bear

Oh, no, I regret nothing. Who knows? Perhaps if things hadn't happened this way, I wouldn't have gone to Barcelona. Anyway, if I had to do it all over, I'd do it exactly the same way.

Over time, I slowly rose through the ranks of Canadian solo swimmers. As I matured, I acquired a bit of the grace that champions need: I could even be artistic from time to time. But good God, although I had been in fairly solid position at the front of the Canadian pack since 1985, I always came in second. Carolyn Waldo was the reigning queen.

At the 1984 Los Angeles Games, synchronized swimming became part of the Olympics. I was happy to see this official recognition of "my" sport. Ranked fifth in Canada at the time, I couldn't participate in those games; anyway, I was so young. But there would be the 1988 Games . . .

Carolyn had won the silver medal in Los Angeles, and she deserved it. Being at the Games infused her with a good dose of confidence, and she was now ready to take the limelight. All the limelight.

She was an uncomplicated girl who was always smiling,

and she was a true swimming machine, strong as an ox and a hard worker. Now, eighteen months before the Seoul games, she was a solid first; I was a solid second. There was no doubt that it was her right to perform the Olympic solo, and her place in the duet could not be questioned. However, this latter event would have given me a chance to go to the Olympics. In my mind, and Julie's, one of the duet spots should be mine; I had worked hard enough for it. But there was a hitch. In Calgary, where she swam, Carolyn already had a duet partner: Michelle Cameron.

For a while, the possibility of sending the two best in compulsories was considered, but this posed a major problem. As the second best, I was the nuisance, the fly in the ointment, the unscrupulous young thing who wanted to break up a marriage that had lasted fifteen years.

Julie was asked to write down why she wanted to break up the pair. "Why not send the two best?" was her response. The Calgary coach, Debbie Muir, was asked to explain why the pair should stay together, and she probably talked about their experience and partnership in the duet.

At the same time, I was being worked on, too. Two and a half months before the qualifications, Pat Murray, then president of Synchro Canada, invited me out for dinner. She wanted me to see that I had very little chance of qualifying. Even if I did, I would have to move to Calgary, buy a car, and so on.

Buy a car! When my mother didn't even have the money to repair hers!

Pat talked and I played with my food. Finally, the decision came out: the pair would remain intact. Michelle was ranked third in Canada, and yet she would be going to Seoul. The most frustrating thing was that I couldn't hate her for it. Among all the Anglophones on the Canadian team, she was the nicest, the most down-to-earth, and surely my best friend.

As a consolation prize, I was invited to the Calgary

training camp. I could even go to Seoul as a substitute, but I would watch the competition from the stands.

"Could I stay in Montreal and train with videotapes you send?" I asked. "I could videotape myself and you could evaluate my work."

No way.

"Could I go a little later so that I can keep working on my solo with Julie?"

No way.

"If I go to Calgary, is there at least a chance that I'll swim with Carolyn at the Games?"

This time, the answer was at least hesitant: "There may be a chance, if your compulsory marks are extremely high . . ."

What they were asking from me was not 100 percent, but 120 percent — to outdo Michelle. Victories in synchronized swimming were won by tenths, even hundredths of a point; I knew that as well as anyone. They didn't want to say no, but in fact that's what they were saying. It was like asking a rookie to score fifteen goals against the Canadiens' goalie during warm-up. For years, I had been beating Michelle by the equivalent of two or three goals, not by twenty. I got the point. Unless Michelle drowned, I wouldn't be swimming at the Olympics.

For me, going to Calgary was like travelling to a foreign country. From one training camp to the next, my English didn't improve much. After a few weeks in "labour camp," as I called them, I knew enough to say, "I don't understand" and to figure out what they meant when they corrected me by saying "You're on your face." In French, we said, "You're on your nose." Nose, face. Nose, face. I didn't see a direct link, but I finally figured out that it meant the same thing: in a vertical position, my legs were inclined toward my face.

Each time I was about to leave for Calgary, I would burst into tears: "Mom, I don't want to go." But I always ended up there, usually with only one other Quebecer, who felt as exiled as I did.

Usually, the coaches mimed the leg movements with their fingers and tried to make me understand what they meant. There were three coaches for ten girls, and nothing escaped their notice. They found six mistakes per pool length.

Those horrid camps. I don't know why, but the water was icy cold. We always got out of the pool with otitis, tendonitis, torn muscles, and an appointment with the physiotherapist.

The ambience wasn't much warmer. We stayed in university residences or, worse, in convents. Frédéric always sent me comics or little jokes to cheer me up. One of François's letters was seven pages long and entitled, "Eighteen Ways to Escape a Convent Without Setting Off the Alarm."

In fact, the problem wasn't getting *out* of the convent, but getting *in*. One time, at a convent where a handicapped nun was the doorkeeper, we came in late, which obliged the poor woman to get out of bed, and we never again dared to stay out past curfew.

Often, I was the soloist. But since I was only fifteen and the other girls were nineteen or twenty, I was the little pain, the spoiled baby. On top of that, I didn't know a single word of English, and so I often panicked. I forgot when I had to take the bus, when I had to go back. Every time someone laughed, I was sure it was at my expense.

I wasn't the only one who felt this uncomfortable. When Julie went with me, she had to coach me in English, so that everyone could understand her. I was the only one who didn't know what she was saying!

To me, training camp in Calgary felt like it was a year long. I would be without my mother, my friends, my school, and my coach . . . and why? To go and cheer on two girls in Seoul.

Not wanting to deprive me of an Olympic experience,

even a passive one, Julie didn't dare say a word. As for Mom, her attitude never changed. "If you want to do it, you keep going. If not, you can give it up. Either way, you'll always be my champion." It was up to me to make the decision, all alone, like a grown-up.

I said no. And then I felt awful.

"What's going on with Karine?" Natou said, worried. I was huddled on the bodybuilding mat, crying my eyes out. Karine was completely gone, leaving behind nothing but a whimpering, pathetic Sylvie, a person the other swimmers had never seen before.

I didn't eat. At school, I did nothing but doodle in my notebooks. I didn't even swim anymore. Julie, desperate to see the Karine she knew again, called on a psychologist, Luc Pelletier, who was to help me later, when Sylvain . . .

Gently, he dug down deep inside of me, beyond the tears, the rage, and the frustration, and asked the essential question: "Why do you swim?"

It took me a moment to react, and then the answer came, clear as a bell: "Because I love it."

Beyond the medals, beyond the victories, beyond even the despair, there was this feeling: "I love to swim." No one could take this passion from me.

As Luc brought me out of my torpor, he also roused Karine: "So, they want you to crack, eh? Well, you'll have to show them what you're really made of. You're going to the Olympics in Barcelona in 1992, and you'll get there under your own steam, too . . ."

And, eagerly, I began to train again, doing my best to transform all my frustration into motivation. Of course, it wasn't always a bowl of cherries. There were days . . .

I had always kept a diary, which I called "My Little Prince." Why, I don't know. Perhaps because of my young cousin Jean-François. After his burial, we all stood around the grave, weeping, while my aunt, Jean-François's mother, read passages from *The Little Prince.* When she got choked up and couldn't go on, my mother or another of my aunts would continue reading.

One day in February 1988, I had a particularly hard time at the pool and, as always, I consoled myself by writing in my diary. "Hi! Today was a tough day. I hit my knee in bodybuilding, my ear hurt in the water, I almost couldn't finish the duet, and my solo was a total mess. My pulse was 198, and normally it's around 154. As you can see, I'm exhausted!"

I was exhausted, true, but I knew I was improving.

In the fall of 1988, I was watching the duet performance at the Olympics on TV with a twinge in my heart, when the doorbell rang. It was Guy Asselin, my neighbour, a police officer with the Quebec Police Force and a shooting champion. Jean-François, his little boy, was holding a bouquet. On the card were the words: "In our heart and in the hearts of all Quebecers, you're our champion."

In spite of placing second in their free program, the Canadians finally won — but just — their gold medal in Seoul. If it hadn't been for Carolyn's solid performance in the compulsories, it would have gotten away.

EIGHT

The Way Is Clear

You can leave in peace now, Carolyn. You can retire. I'm ready. It's my turn now!

Year after year, month after month, I was improving. I was winning competitions in other countries, but never at home, never when Carolyn was there.

After the 1988 Olympics, Carolyn retired. She had done everything she had set out to do: a silver medal at the 1984 Los Angeles Olympic Games, two gold medals, in solo and duet, at Seoul, not to mention her world titles. What more could an athlete ask?

With her gone, my way was clear. Finally, I could hold my head up. For years, that was what had bothered me the most: never feeling that I was the best. I represented Canada, but I wasn't even the champion in my country. In my heart of hearts, I wasn't able to stand tall with my head high. Now that she had retired, it was different.

"What do you think of Carolyn Waldo?" asked Mr. Chapleau, my anatomy professor at university, who liked to tease me. But this time, I didn't see his trap.

"Carolyn and I are very different, but I like her, and I respect her as an athlete," I told him.

Mr. Chapleau smiled: "Haven't you seen the article in *La Presse?*"

No, I hadn't seen it. I finally found a copy of the newspaper, in the cafeteria, I think. In a short article, Carolyn was announcing to the public that I would never be a world champion because I didn't have what it takes.

At first, her remarks made me sad: "Why is she spitting on me like that? She's had everything she wants, so she should give me a chance to prove myself."

Karine got the ball rolling from there: "So, show her what you can do!"

I started training with even more enthusiasm than ever.

Dear Mr. Chapleau. I admit that I could have done without his sarcasm, but I liked him. Not all my professors were so kind.

Combining sports and studies is an impossible juggling act. They were talking about sports-study programs at the time, but there was nothing really definite yet.

Throughout elementary and even high school, everything went perfectly. Synchronized swimming took up less time, as did my schoolwork. And then Mom, who was a wizard at French and math, kept a close eye on me, too. She would even circle spelling and grammar mistakes in my messages and make me correct them later. When I was finished my lessons and homework, I couldn't go straight outside and play. I still had to go through a series of flash cards with arithmetic problems on one side, the solution on the other.

My attachment to Mom made me vulnerable. From time to time, at Stella-Maris High School, a tough kid would shove me against the lockers: "Hey, you mama's girl." Yes, I was a mama's girl. It was as clear as spring water. We didn't have much money — not enough to buy jeans, like the other girls could. Mom made mine, but she forgot to put the pockets on the seat. And a comb in the back pocket was simply essential! But I didn't have one.

Still, I did well and was near the top of my class. Mom's discipline bore fruit. For my last year of high school, I moved to an enriched class at Joseph-François-Perreault School. The principal, Mr. Beaulieu, a small white-haired man, seemed very happy to see me. "So, you do synchronized swimming?" he asked at our first meeting. From time to time, when I missed a test because of a competition, he let me do a make-up or just used my average.

In college, things weren't so easy. Even though I was a long-time member of the Canadian team, there was no question of exempting me from the physical-education courses. When I got back from the Australia Games, a professor had given me a zero in math, since I'd missed the two exams and there was no possibility of a make-up test.

From that point on, my physics professor helped me choose my courses, not on the basis of my preferences or abilities, but according to which teachers would be most understanding, most forgiving.

In the end, it took me four years instead of two to get my college diploma, with an average of almost eighty percent. It was while I was at college that I realized I couldn't be a doctor — at least, not a swimmer and a doctor. It was one or the other. In fact, to get into medical school, I would have needed marks of ninety-five percent in all subjects. What a disappointment!

Time was slipping through my fingers. There were my studies, there were five hours of training per day. But that wasn't all. There were also money problems.

When we were small, we had to sell chocolate bars or collect sponsors for swim-a-thons and synchro-thons to help finance the club. Often, boys who played hockey, a much more popular sport in Rosemont, had knocked on the doors before me. And since I was the only club swimmer in the neighbourhood, I made my rounds alone. But the classes weren't too expensive, and Mom cheerfully scraped together the money to pay for them.

Later, when I was at college, then university, the problems got bigger. Swimming at the elite level was something else. The cost of membership in my club, which now included all trips, had multiplied. When we got onto the national team, we received a letter of congratulations — "Welcome to the team" — and a bill. I didn't pay the nine hundred dollars in 1992, perhaps because I represented Canada in Barcelona.

As well as doing my own training, I began to coach to make ends meet. I would get to the pool at two in the afternoon, and I didn't leave until nine at night. And I hadn't yet eaten or studied.

Having put aside my dream of being a doctor, I registered for a course that seemed related but that I was sure would be easier: physical education.

I was wrong. I, who had always been at the top of my class, was ashamed of my marks, which were around average or just above. Average! Mom had trained me never to settle for average.

The pedagogical aspect didn't interest me, but the physiology did: I was fascinated with psychomotor development in infants, for example, and how babies progress. I love children so much. Even today, if one comes over, I take out my dolls and slip back into childhood: googoo! Newborns, however, intimidate me. I want a dozen children, but I always tell Mom that she'll have to take care of them during the very first months. It scares me too much. Mom always laughs when I say this.

At university, my crutch was my cousin Manon. The day before exams, I would ask her, "Manon, can I borrow your notes?" Sometimes, when I stumbled over a difficult section, I called her. Then I went to the exam . . . and passed.

I was so used to cramming that eventually I couldn't

study normally anymore. Although there were times when I was away and had to miss my classes, there were also moments of respite. But since I was used to working in top gear, using my textbooks and the notes of a bunch of friends, I found ordinary classes boring, so I doodled instead of taking notes.

Dear Manon. When I see her, I never know what to say. Since I became world champion, I get offered a job in every school I visit. Me, who had average marks and didn't even finish my B.A. Meanwhile, with her excellent marks and her honestly earned degree, Manon, like most young people her age, can't find a job in her field.

I chose to swim. Obviously, this wouldn't last forever, I knew, but I would think about the future after the Olympics.

In Paris in 1989, I represented Canada for the first time with my head held high. I participated in the World Cup as Canadian champion, *the* Canadian champion.

I stepped onto the podium three times: for the bronze medal in duet with Natou, for the silver team medal, and for the silver in solo.

I was proud. The American swimmer, Tracey Long, may have gone home with the gold medal, but I'd swum well. When the results were announced, the spectators threw their programs into the pool, and some even booed. Throughout the competition, in fact, the marks had been a little strange, with bizarre fluctuations. My earphones on, isolated in my bubble, I had decided to block out the negative vibes. I was happy with my performance; I had done my best, and that was the important thing.

But now the prestige of synchronized swimming was on the rise. As an Olympic sport, it was drawing a new audience. While I was on the way home, the telephone was ringing off the hook at Julie's, at home, and at the pool: "What's wrong with Sylvie? Doesn't she have what it takes to win?" Obviously, the Canadian journalists didn't share my view of things.

In various ways, more or less adroitly, they all asked the

same question. In the next day's newspapers, the message was the same: "Sylvie disappointing."

Shit!

I had read through the articles and was so angry that I wouldn't touch a reporter with a ten-foot pole, when the telephone rang yet again. "Another journalist!" I said to myself. It was true. A television journalist this time, from RDS, the Quebec sports network.

It was Sylvain Lake.

NINE

Marvellous Macho!

I know, I know. The Olympic people are waiting so they can present the medals. But my hair is all slimy, I've got gel all over me, and I want to change swimsuits. I've been running my whole life. Now it's over. They can wait a little. After all, they can't present the medals without me . . .

Behind my gentle, polite façade is a bit of a rebel. Nothing really delinquent, just Karine's voice, instead of mine, from time to time answering: "Now, that's enough!" Most of the time, I didn't say anything, just shook my head.

With Sylvain, it was different. The journalists' criticisms, their saying that perhaps Carolyn was right, perhaps I was destined always to come in second — it was too much. Shaken up by their cold reception, Karine had just sounded the battle cry when Sylvain arrived in my life. His timing couldn't have been worse, and he got what I was thinking right in the face. This happened four years ago, but I remember it like it was yesterday.

"Oh, you journalists, you're all the same, you can't even recognize a good performance. And something artistic like synchronized swimming isn't really a sport to you. All you see is a pair of legs and a girl with make-up. You're a bunch of machos! Besides, I wear almost no make-up. So there!"

Sylvain let the storm blow for a while. Then, when I paused for breath, he protested, "Listen, Sylvie, I'm an athlete, too. I understand."

I calmed down a bit. Finally, we made an agreement. I would grant him an interview for RDS in a few days.

Some of the girls had heard about him: nice mouth, beautiful eyes, but a damned macho . . . And then, in his book, *Le cauchemar olympique (The Olympic Nightmare)*, he had written about the incompetents in synchronized swimming, and had even claimed that there was drug use. What drugs? Surely not steroids — we would sink like stones.

"I haven't eaten supper," he said just before the interview.

Without thinking, I retorted, "You live on love and fresh water?"

"No, just fresh water . . ."

I wasn't really in the mood for frivolousness. I had one thing to tell this guy, and I wasn't going to let the opportunity pass. What did he mean, drugs in synchronized swimming? First, what did he know about synchronized swimming? Then, what was the idea of criticizing something he knew almost nothing about?

I talked in his face, as they say. When he asked me, smiling, if I'd read *Le cauchemar olympique*, I had to admit that I hadn't. Touché! I hadn't had the time. I would certainly read it a little later, but not before Christmas. With my training and my studies, I was too busy.

But I finished reading it by the next day. I even talked about it in an interview at radio station CKAC.

That very day, Sylvain called: "It seems you had time to read it before Christmas after all."

We saw each other again. Over hot chocolate and a

muffin, we talked sports, injuries, competitions. He had been a four-hundred-metre runner, and had even represented Canada at the World University Games in 1987. Yes, he had suffered like I had. He understood.

"He's not bad. He'd make a nice boyfriend for you," my mother commented.

I said, "No, no." And to Sylvain, using my swimming and studies as an excuse and reproaching him for his lack of seriousness, his reputation as a runner, I also said, "No, no." One day, he pointed at the sky and said, "Look up. It's written in heaven that we'll be together one day."

"Damned macho!"

He smiled at my insult.

I didn't really believe it. He might have been macho, even arrogant, with others, but never with me.

I left for the Commonwealth Games with my bags full of surprises. I would be away for more than a month. Sylvain had prepared presents, one for each day, which I couldn't unwrap until the date marked on it. One was candy, another was a little note, yet another was chewing gum . . .

Mom always told me, "The day you meet the right man, you won't need to wonder, you'll know."

I was lying on her bed, half asleep, and she was stroking my hair, when I admitted to her, "Mom, it's him, I know it."

Mom felt like she'd been slapped. It had happened. She would soon have to share her big daughter.

A little earlier, I would have felt like I was abandoning her, but she'd been seeing Jean-Pierre for some time now. He was the first man to come into her life since Papa's death. She had always said, "I'll never have another man in my life unless I meet one who's as good as your father was." And she never did, until she met Jean-Pierre, a widower.

When I came back from the Commonwealth Games, Sylvain and I decided to live together. Papa had left me a little money, which would provide us with the means to set up house.

Romantics would probably describe our first apartment as a little love nest. We called it our closet. I couldn't even stretch my legs without hitting a piece of furniture.

It didn't take long for us to move in. I brought an artificial Christmas tree and my swimsuits. Sylvain had a popcorn machine.

The Hochelaga-Maisonneuve neighbourhood wasn't very safe at night, so, when Sylvain had to work late, I slept with the poker beside the bed. Yes, our closet had a fireplace. Romantic, eh? There was just one problem: the apartment was so small that the tiniest fire turned it into a furnace.

We hardly saw each other. As the junior broadcaster at RDS, he had the night shift, and he rarely got home before three in the morning, while I was always studying or training.

It wasn't always easy. Sometimes at night I felt like I was gasping for air. I was suffocating, literally. This would happen before a competition in which I had to execute a very difficult routine. I dreamed that I was underwater and couldn't get to the surface. Or I found myself on the shore of a river and I had to do my routine there, but I couldn't see anything, not even the bottom. On these nights, Sylvain would wake me up and speak to me softly, and I would begin to breathe again.

Since my "disappointing" defeat at the World Cup, I hadn't been beaten. This had its down side, however. My routines had become very demanding, heading more and more toward perfection and taking me to the limits of my strength. Now, it was time to try for the world championship.

TEN

Two Boubous at the World Championships

Shit! Just one defeat in three years, and it had to happen here at the Games. And in this way! And that never-ending American anthem — it's like turning the knife in the wound. I don't understand it. These are the Olympics; the games are for us, the athletes. Why is the American anthem played all the way through every time, while the others run only forty-five seconds? Is it really because the Americans put more money into the Games, as we've been told?

The Americans have always tripped me up.

For months, Julie had been preparing me for the 1991 world championships in Perth, Australia. My arch-rival was Kristen Babb.

"Watch her walk, watch her smile," Julie told me. "You'll have to beat her outside the pool, not in the water."

Kristen was a marvel. She didn't just walk into a room, she made an entrance. Her big hats, brilliant smile, and Dior model looks were much admired, and her kindness won hearts.

Everyone liked Kristen, including me. Beside her, I looked like an ugly duckling. Happily, I caught up to her in the pool.

"Look at you: you've got one shoulder higher than the other, you wear rubber thongs, and you're so shy," Julie scolded. "You don't talk to anyone, and the judges don't even know who you are."

"But Julie, what can I say to them? I don't know them. And besides, I can hardly speak English."

But Julie didn't lay off me. She forced me to walk gracefully, to hold myself erect, to talk to the Canadian judges while they were waiting for the international officials.

"Julie, I do want to be more graceful in my performances," I protested, "but I can't be a boot licker."

"All I am asking you to do is say hello and look like someone who knows how to enjoy life," she told me. "If you want to be a champion, you have to act like one, not just perform like one. That's what's missing."

When I arrived at the outdoor pool in Perth, I froze. On the other side, Kristen was shining on the universe, as bright as the sun. She was doing her warm-up exercises as everyone looked on full of admiration.

"You know what you have to do," Julie told me. "Go and see her. She's stretching, so you stretch, too."

"I don't want to do it. Don't make me."

Julie didn't say another word. So, like someone diving into the water for the first time, I gave her a salute and said, "Yes, boss!"

If Kristen had been doing anything else, I wouldn't have had any ammunition. But she was stretching. I shook her hand, we chatted for a minute, and then I began to stretch, too. I knew that no one could match my flexibility — it was my home advantage. One foot on a chair, I did the splits, as I had done so often in my living room, and then I talked.

Seeing her a little taken aback, slightly irritated, gave me courage. Perhaps this would work, after all.

974: the first Rosemont pool team. Our coach was Ginette Rupp, and that's me, second from left.

tawa, June 1982: My coach, Julie Sauvé, and me, junior national champion.

September 1984: The CAMO team's famous lift in Japan.
That's Martine Labelle we're holding.

September 1984: CAMO team members in front of Buddha. From left:
Catherine Paradis, Danielle Bélanger, Nathalie Guay, and Nathalie Roy.

▪mber 1984: The CAMO team poses in show swimsuits, to the delight of hotel
s. From left: Chantal Laviolette, Catherine Paradis, Nathalie Guay, Penny and
Vicky Vilagos, Martine Labelle, Nathalie Roy, Danielle Bélanger, and me.

Monaco, May 1985: Prince Albert hands out souvenirs.

May 1986: Martine Labelle (head underwater) and Nathalie Guay
during a team lift.

Madrid, August 1986: The Canadian water-polo and synchronized-swimming teams at the world championships. I'm in the first row, second from right.

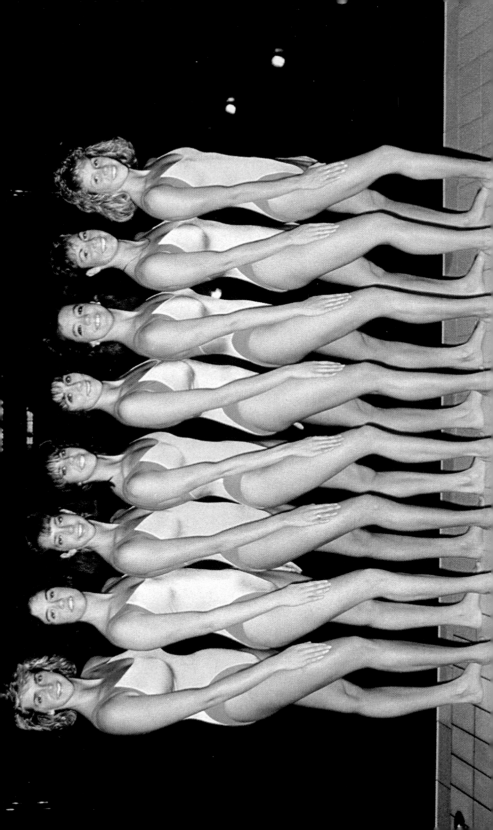

June 1988: Roma Synchro.

June 1988: Roma Synchro.

June 1988: Roma Synchro. Nathalie Guay and I win the gold medal.

The bodybuilding had done its job. I was taller, stronger, and more muscular than she was; when I stood right beside her, the difference showed every time I moved. It really hadn't occurred to me until that moment.

We were still stretching when some coaches from other countries went to see Julie: "Not a bad strategy. It's brilliant to put them side by side like that."

No one could believe that the move hadn't been premeditated.

In the minds of many, I was already world champion, and I hadn't even swum yet.

The last few competitions, I had been talking to the officials, even the Russian judge, who was always so intimidating and so hard on the Canadian girls. Oh, nothing much — just a hello, a smile.

Julie wanted to leave nothing to chance. "You have to make even your practices exceptional," she insisted. "No one must see you as anything but perfect."

But the practice just before the compulsories was awful. The wind was blowing terribly, robbing us of all precision. At one point, a gust even tore down a billboard, which severed the Russian coach's Achilles' tendon. It was horrible; we had no control at all in this wind. I didn't know what to do.

"Swim closer to the wall," Julie whispered. "You'll be more protected from the wind. You're not supposed to swim so close, but there's no actual rule . . ." And she added, "Wait till the wind dies down."

"Competitor number eight!"

It was the third call, but I hadn't budged. Doing my "egg beaters," I stayed right in front of the judges, who were obviously waiting for me to stretch out, as planned, to begin the first figure. When I think about it, it was a very stubborn thing to do. But I looked at the water, kept my eye on the wind . . . and waited. The judges, incredulous and uncomprehending, stared at this big idiot who just kept right on treading water as though she had nothing better to do, who didn't even have the good grace to begin when she was supposed to. Then, suddenly, the wind died down. I stretched out, a little closer to the inside wall, as Julie had advised, so that I didn't toss in the waves like the other competitors.

After the compulsories, with six almost perfect figures, I was leading by three points. To lose, I would have to almost drown when I performed my routine. Instead of reassuring me, this scared me: "I'm too far ahead; it's not right. What's going to happen in my routine?"

I wanted to win this world championship without leaving any doubt that I deserved the title. A true champion doesn't just win the compulsories; she must also win the long program.

I was ready, physically and psychologically. For some time, I'd been performing my championship routine in Europe. We had tried out different music, and the audience invariably began to clap their hands in time to the the Spanish music. I wore my hair in a low bun, like a flamenco dancer. Yes, I knew they'd like the routine.

A few days before, Sylvain had decided to come and join me. It was pure folly. He had paid two thousand dollars for a ticket, while we were scratching for pennies. Nevertheless, I was happy that he was coming. I loved him for being so romantic, impulsive, and a little crazy.

But would he get there in time? His plane landed at three o'clock, and I was swimming at four; his trip halfway around the world would have taken twenty-four hours; there were a number of stopovers, and the slightest hitch could turn into a long delay.

I had asked that a ticket in his name be left at the box office. While I was waiting my turn in the tent, I looked for him — and kept an ear out, too. I knew I would hear him the minute he arrived. He would shout our special signal: "Boubou! Boubou!"

He started calling me Boubou, the French word for grumpy, the very first time he saw me in a bad mood. And I called him Boubou, too, for the same reason. To our families, we had become the two Boubous.

But I couldn't hear anything.

"Karine, concentrate."

It was very hot, at least 40°C. The pool deck felt like a bed of glowing coals as I walked across it. Ouch! It would have been nice to walk on the slightly cooler synthetic carpet. The tension was palpable. "Bring on the pressure," I said to myself. "I know that it makes me even better."

I swam very well. As planned, the audience was swept away, and so were the seven judges. Out of fourteen marks, I received seven perfect tens. My score of 201.013 points erased Carolyn Waldo's world record. I wasn't just world champion, I'd beaten her mark, and this meant everything to me.

For years, even after Carolyn retired, I was always being compared to her when I won international competitions as Canadian champion. "Carolyn did it like this, Carolyn didn't do that," people would mutter.

After Perth, I was more accepted. I wasn't Carolyn, and I never would be. I was Sylvie, and perhaps that was finally enough. I felt like a weight had been lifted from my shoulders. Now I was world champion, the best in the world.

As I was leaving the stadium, the gold medal around my neck, an employee came up to me. "Are you Sylvie Fréchette? There is someone here for you."

It was Sylvain! His plane had stopped on every little island between Canada and Australia, and he had missed everything. But he was there. He cried out, looked at my medal, then hugged me very tight.

At the hotel, I was the only one with something to celebrate. The other Canadians, both duet and team, hadn't yet swum their finals, but with the duet in third place and the team in second after the preliminaries, they had no hope of victory; the gap was too wide for them to close.

As the only Francophone, I hadn't wanted to train with the team before the championships. I didn't want to go to Calgary for six months without Julie, whom I considered the best coach in the world. Since Julie couldn't leave the rest of the club to go with me, I had chosen to stay home and work on my solo, close to Mom and my family. The other girls had their own opinion of this: I hadn't made any sacrifices for them, and yet I was the only one to get a gold medal. That was more than enough to be depressed about.

When we left the restaurant, we were confronted by an army of cockroaches. Ugh! Bugs terrified me. Sylvain, who had no fear of insects, teased me gently. In fact, snakes were his only phobia.

The phone in our hotel room never stopped ringing. In Quebec, they had just discovered Sylvie Fréchette, world champion. Every radio host at CKAC alone wanted to talk to me live. For almost my entire career, no one had paid much attention to synchronized swimming, so refusing was out of the question. Anyway, in spite of a little tantrum in Germany, I liked journalists. They had always been kind to me; in fact, some of my best friends . . .

Sylvain and I had just a few days to spend together at the other end of the world. When the interviews were over, we decided to go on a honeymoon. There was a peaceful spot, Rottnest Island, where bicycles were the only mode of transportation. We had to get there by boat. Strange as it may seem, I'm scared of boats. Even with my fourteen life jackets well buckled, I began to cry.

"Look, look over there," Sylvain said excitedly. "It's following the boat!"

He was pointing behind us. Then I saw it: a dolphin, my symbolic animal. With my nose glued to the window, I laughed through my tears like a little girl who'd just seen Santa Claus — or, better, Flipper. It was him: Flipper. For the entire fifteen-minute ride, I laughed and cried at the same time.

The island was magnificent. Unfortunately, most of the beaches were inaccessible, protected by a dense wall of vegetation. But in the end we found a small beach surrounded by magnificent dunes that were more like ramparts than walls. The soft, warm sand ran like flour through our fingers. We were just like kids, rolling in the sand and climbing the dunes, which disintegrated under our feet.

All the fun and games made us thirsty, and we wanted a glass of wine. Near the restaurant, a huge sign said: BEWARE OF THE SNAKES! And below, in slightly smaller letters: "Watch out for sand snakes. Do not dig, as it brings them out. This snake's bite is fatal."

I felt Sylvain cringe. In an instant, he hated Australia. Instead of staying on for a few weeks after I left, as planned, he decided to leave the country as soon as possible. Besides, the Gulf War had just been declared. His return trip was more circuitous than mine, and he was worried that the war might disrupt his itinerary, so he left.

But Julie wanted to see a kangaroo before leaving Australia. How could we go to Australia and not see a kangaroo? We rented a car and took off. After three and a half hours of driving, we finally arrived at a beach. The ocean was wild, but a few surfers were still up to the challenge.

On the way back, we were stopped by the police. Not only was Julie speeding, but it turned out that she had forgotten her driver's licence. The police officers patiently repeated, "Too fast! Too fast!" But Julie just stared at them in bewilderment, answering in French that she didn't understand anything. Julie, who spoke English so well! Finally, they let us go without a ticket, without even a warning.

An hour later, we were back at the hotel, without having seen a single kangaroo either.

I wanted to stop in Fiji on the way home. Just the name meant heaven on earth to me: Fiji, the banana islands! But the beach was brown, the water dirty, and the capital looked like a Third World city. Where was the postcard island with its banana trees?

Julie and I chose an island to visit. We could walk all the way around it, they had told us. So as not to weigh ourselves down, we left some of our things on the beach. After ten minutes, Julie looked at me: "That's strange, this looks just like the other side." Then we saw our things and understood. We had walked around the island in ten minutes! Damn!

Our homecoming at Dorval Airport was a party. Friends, neighbours, and journalists were all waiting for me at the exit. In all the excitement, I didn't even notice that Grandma Charbonneau wasn't there. She was suffering from angina, and couldn't take part in the celebration.

A few days later, there was a reception for me in the gymnasium of my elementary school, École Saint-François-Solano. On the wall was a picture they had made of a girl in a bikini swimming among fish. There were fish everywhere. Every group of students had prepared a presentation. One little first-grader had even been dressed up in a swimsuit and hairdo identical to what I had worn for my first Canadian championship.

My old teachers stared wide-eyed at me. Obviously, they had never made the connection between their old student and the synchronized-swimming champion. I laughed.

A letter asking for donations had gone out, and the parents had contributed eight hundred dollars, which a pair of twins gave me in a large red-velvet purse. "To help you continue training," they explained.

On my return from Perth, *Le Journal de Montréal* had published an article with a page-wide headline: "Champion penniless." Judging by the reaction, a lot of people read it. A cleaner even offered me ten dollars to attend the opening of his store.

I earned my "Boubou" nickname more than ever when the telephone rang for what seemed like the thousandth time.

Sylvain ran for the phone: "I'll take your calls . . ."

And that's how he became my agent.

ELEVEN

Karine Takes Over

Sylvain was tireless. In addition to his career as a television reporter, he was preparing for the Barcelona Olympic Games — both mine and his, since he had been asked to be the analyst for the track-and-field events. In his rare free moments, he took care of my career, setting up appointments for me, trying to get me sponsors. He had even committed himself to writing my biography . . . but where was Karine's?

Karine was taking up more and more room. Sometimes, she collided head-on with "my" manager, and then each stubbornly held on, pulling on his or her end of the blanket. But in the end the two Boubous intervened, and Sylvie and Sylvain re-emerged more in love than ever. Between training sessions and reporting assignments, we squeezed in a moonlit walk, a candlelit dinner. I barely knew how to boil an egg, so Sylvain always did the cooking.

No, that's not true. There was one time . . .

I decided to make chicken. I had never had the time to cook, nor even to learn how. When I got home from the market, I took a good look at the funny-looking bird. Buying it was the easy part, but now what was I going to do with it?

I called Mom. She laughed. "Start by taking off the wrapping . . ."

When the chicken finally came out of the oven, plump and golden, I ran to get the camera to catch it on film for posterity. Sylvain posed proudly with my trophy, his hungry mouth wide open.

Between our careers and our life together, there wasn't much time for anything else. I even saw Mom on the fly.

Since I'd become Canadian champion, my routines had gained in dramatic intensity. I was finally beginning to dare to express myself. After all, now that I was champion, I could allow myself some self-confidence. Gradually, almost unnoticed, Karine separated from little Sylvie, who was too shy for her taste, and took over. Her bold moves sometimes made officials gulp and brought a smile to my lips.

In 1989, I competed in an orange-pink swimsuit. The colour was quite loud, even a little shocking, but there was more. A magnificent lightning bolt, made of transparent fabric, zigzagged down between my breasts! It was unheard-of! The committee in charge of approving swimsuits didn't know what to do.

Inside, a little voice was tickling me. "Karine," I thought, "don't make me laugh. This isn't the time."

Before the wide-eyed judges, I forced myself to be un-provocative, as angelic as possible. They must see only Sylvie, and not Karine. Finally, they grudgingly accepted it. Nothing in the rules forbade transparent fabric. The next year, the rules were amended.

On the other hand, the reaction in Barcelona warmed my heart. I immediately felt that they liked the lace, and I'm sure that we will see it often in the future. Perhaps people will even copy the opening in the back, like a half-open window on the muscles well defined by bodybuilding. My swimsuits always fit like a second skin; if they moved a quarter of an inch, I took them in. The swimsuit for the Games required more than a hundred hours of work. With the bustier, which got rid of the eternal shoulder straps, and the lace, it was a lot for the officials to digest all at once. We took a chance, but I think we won. They loved it.

But what a road I had to travel to get to those Games . . .

Far from discouraging Karine, the second place at the World Cup in Paris spurred her on. The journalists' reaction probably helped, too. Karine was getting bolder and bolder. Julie, who had always complained about my shyness, now took a wicked pleasure in fanning the flame. Swept up in the heat of the moment, I began to have fun, too.

I was always looking for something different in the unusual sounds and rhythms of New Age, alternative, and even heavy metal music. A skeptical Martin spent entire evenings recording music at my request, editing out one bit, splicing in another. Sometimes, he came up with something so crazy, so bizarre, that it would surely please his big sister. And it pleased me no matter what.

I had fun pushing the rules to their limits and turning conventions upside down. I was the first to swim to music with French words. Against all expectations, "Le rêve de Stella Spotlight," from the rock opera *Starmania*, pleased the judges. "It reflects your culture well," they told me.

However, there were still many barriers to overcome, and some of them were huge. It was at the 1990 Commonwealth Games that I dared not to smile for the very first time.

It was an unwritten rule, but a stricter one than any on the books, that a synchronized swimmer must smile. It showed that she was enjoying herself, having fun, and, especially, *especially*, it hid her fatigue or suffering. The absence of a smile was unfailingly interpreted as proof of weakness. Without their smiles, most swimmers would have felt naked. I always detested this artificial, immobile smile, even during the most dramatic music. If I didn't try, who would?

To make it work, it was essential that I choose music that

would make the slightest smile seem inappropriate. So I swam to "Amazing Grace," sung by Nana Mouskouri. The music was exquisite, poignant, arousing fervor and emotion, but certainly not smiles.

In Auckland, New Zealand, I earned a perfect mark of ten for the first time for my interpretation of "Amazing Grace." Also for the first time, three judges admitted to me that seeing me swim brought tears to their eyes. Yes, I could move people, touch their hearts.

After the world championships, Karine was truly unleashed. Fortified by the championship crown, she went wild, deciding to revolutionize synchronized swimming. Nothing could stop her — neither fear, nor ridicule, nor Julie, and certainly not me. But I was having too much fun to think about reining her in.

For the first time, for the 1991 World Cup, in Bonn, Germany, the International Federation had decided that a short program would be presented in addition to the long program, a little like figure skating. So Julie and I immediately thought of the Duchesnays, the figure-skating revolutionaries. A short program was an invitation to originality.

We agreed right away: "We'll push the artistic aspect to the max . . . We'll need special music and a special swimsuit."

We had seen gymnast Stella Umeh, at the Canadian championships, perform a routine to the sound of tom-toms. That gave us an idea.

We made a rough sketch, but we had to find the right movements. "Just put on the music and let me do something," I told Julie. "You'll tell me if it looks good."

Our best discoveries often came to us as we played. I would get into the water and do any crazy movement that went through my mind. And often a spark would be struck. A little movement, a bit of mime . . .

We tried to imagine native people around a fire, stooped over, a slightly threatening feeling . . . For the occasion, I

would wear a special swimsuit, a very special one. Only
Frédéric would understand. Frédéric was one of the design-
ers for the swimsuit company. When they saw me coming with
one of my extravagant ideas, they unfailingly sent me to
Frédéric, saying, "He'll take care of it." And, indeed, he was
the only one who could take what existed in my imagination
and bring it to life in a swimsuit design.

This time, yet again, he understood. He made me a brown
swimsuit, with leaves and flowers and a vine for a shoulder
strap. As for my hair, a long brown braid emerged from a bun
to emphasize my head turns at the dramatic parts of the music.
My eyes were made up with black liner to bring out the whites
of my anxious eyes, attentive to the slightest sound in the jungle
around me.

Crazy! Completely crazy! But, after all, my long program
would be performed to very classical Beethoven, so I could
surely allow myself a few fantasies in the short program. To
tell the truth, it was more fun and a more stimulating
challenge. In fact, anyone could swim to Beethoven, but the
beat of the tom-toms was something else. And it could have
been worse. At first, I had thought about extending the
swimsuit down one thigh and finishing the leg with a ragged
border. I also wanted to wear an armband. But, fearing that
the officials would faint dead away, we pulled back a little —
luckily, as it turned out.

When the time came to present the routine to the
Canadian judges to get an idea of the officials' reactions, we
were a little uncertain.

In unison, the judges said "Yuck!"

But while the judges couldn't find the words to describe
this unnameable spectacle, the swimmers were unanimous:
"Go ahead! It's great!" They adored it.

Finally, Julie said, "Why not be creative? You're the world
champion. They'll respect you."

When she saw the other girls line up for the short

program, Julie was paralyzed. In the middle of the little buns, the sequins, the candy pink and pale green, I couldn't have looked more out of place. Tarzan or, worse, Cheetah in the court of Versailles.

Julie didn't say anything, but she couldn't help thinking, "This time, Julie, you really blew it . . . it's more than a bomb, it's an atom bomb! What came over us?" If I had known what was going through her mind, I surely would have panicked. But it was much too late for her to say anything to me. For the moment, as the wild girl among the ladies, I wasn't uncomfortable; I simply thought I was original.

When I jumped into the water for my warm-up, all the swimmers got out of the pool. As I finished, I heard them applauding. With the judges, however, it was a different story. If it hadn't been for my performance to dear Mr. Beethoven, I no doubt would have lost my title. My little expedition into the jungle could have cost me very dearly.

Several teams had tried to use a theme before this, but such experiments hadn't been continued. I was the world champion. In the minds of the athletes, coaches, and judges, I had the right to spearhead styles. The following year, a number of swimmers chose to put together a real choreography, with a theme. Here and there, one could hear tom-toms. It warmed my heart; it was the best kind of compliment.

TWELVE

Picasso, Dali, van Gogh, and Shakespeare

Since the world championships, Sylvain and I were doing a little better financially. I had received a little sponsorship money from Dr. Scholl, and the government was giving me a grant of $650 per month. What a fortune!

It was Sylvain who found the condo of our dreams. It was by the river, immense and full of light, with a large bedroom up on the third floor — big enough for us to have some space . . .

I had been bugging him for quite a while: Julie had two cats, the Vilagos twins had a couple, too; why not me? In fact, Annie's cat had just had a litter. Boubou! Just two tiny cats to keep me company?

Sylvain was scared of cats; his fondest dream was to cook his parents' cat, Ti-Mine, in the microwave. Up to now, he'd had an excuse: "We live in a closet, it's too small . . ."

But now, in our new home, I could answer his protest: "Oh, Boubou! Just two tiny little cats. I'll take care of them."

Julie also launched an assault: "Could I give her two for her birthday? It would make her so happy."

Julie loved animals. She had a large, hairy English sheep-dog named Fafouin, who was quite a scatterbrain. A big, furry bear. She was crazy about him. Over the years, she brought Fafouin to the pool from time to time, though she had to lock him in the changing room for fear that he'd jump into the water with us. When he died, hit by a car, she cried for weeks, and couldn't hide her grief. On the other hand, when she got divorced, nothing in her attitude let on what had happened, and it wasn't until three years later that we learned the truth when one of us, a little curious, wondered aloud why we hadn't seen her husband recently.

Blessed Julie always put us in a quandary; she tried to dissuade all of her engaged girls from making the big leap, from "getting hooked," as she put it. It didn't matter where we were or whether the engaged girl was a complete unknown, Julie threw herself into her apoplectic diatribe. And I'm sure that her ex-husband did the same thing. Julie always has been and always will be married to synchronized swimming above all, and mother to dozens of girls who depend on her alone.

Sylvain and I were getting ready to move into our new palace when Annie — that is, Catherine — arrived at the pool with a box in her arms. "Here, Karine, this is for you," she said. "Choose the two you want."

When I saw the little balls of fur, I realized that Sylvain had said yes. "Oh, Sylvain!"

At first, they all looked like they came out of a Cottonelle commercial, but it didn't take long to figure out which was which.

Because she was all splashes of colour, I named the first one Picasso. The other one was so funny — a haughty little princess, but utterly crazy. She chased her shadow and ran head-first into the wall. I had just seen an exhibition by a great

Spanish master. His long mustache, noble and disdainful air, eccentricity, and even folly resembled my little cat, so I named her Dali.

Sylvain was categorical: "Those cats sleep in the garage." But he was soon playing with them, too. From time to time, I would walk in on him patting them and throwing balls for them. He looked like a little boy caught in the act.

One day, Picasso disappeared. I was in training camp in Montreal, but I couldn't think about swimming. My sweet, affectionate Picasso! She'd been declawed and would surely be devoured by one of the many wild groundhogs and raccoons that prowled around our place.

I wandered like a soul in pain: Picasso! Picasso! As I walked through the neighbourhood, I wept and shook her little toys. She always came running at the sound of the bells. Why wasn't she coming?

Sylvain made posters and put them up everywhere: "Lost cat . . ."

The next evening, he said, "Come on, let's try to find her." We drove into the high grass that bordered the river. I was hoping that Picasso's eyes would be lit up by the headlights and shine in the dark. But no, nothing!

In desperation, I put her food out on the front stairs. After all, how else would she know which house was hers? I placed her cat litter beside it. "She'll smell it, I'm sure." At the pool, the girls laughed at this story for months. But even today, I'm convinced it made all the difference.

When I turned around to see if Sylvain was behind me, I saw my cat coming out of the shrubbery. After a little more than forty-eight hours outside, she was missing a little fur at the end of her tail, but she had all her parts. And a little something extra . . .

A few days later, I began to scratch my stomach and legs. I had been invaded by fleas. Sylvain laughed: "The fleas love you because you have the personality of a dog . . ."

After her adventure, Picasso was never the same. Once so affectionate, she became wilder, more ferocious. Obviously, I'll never know what happened to her during those two days, but our cats were really part of the family after that.

In early March, 1992, I was walking in the door, home from a competition in Germany, lugging my large suitcase, when I heard Sylvain yell, "Quick, close the door!"

I had been away for weeks. "That's a strange way to welcome me home," I was about to retort, but the words never left my lips. Two little balls of fur were struggling down the stairs.

"What's that?"

Sylvain blushed a little: "It was a surprise . . ."

I was at a complete loss. "But Sylvain . . . four cats! And you're the one who doesn't like cats."

"It's different, now," he replied.

That's how van Gogh and Shakespeare came into our life.

The adoption was more difficult for Picasso and Dali, who were clearly unwilling to let the little intruders take their place. Six hours after they arrived, the kittens were still hiding under a sofa. "Don't worry," the veterinarian reassured me. "They have to re-establish the hierarchy." And after a few days and a few scratches, everything calmed down.

Van Gogh, the only male, always has his head under the tap, showing a suspicious love of water. In fact, all my cats like water. Dali, as crazy as ever, tries to catch the smallest drop, and I have to fight with the two others to keep them from coming into the shower with me. Invariably, whenever the water is running, I see their four little noses stuck to the steamed-up glass.

Frankly, I prefer to keep my cats in sight. Otherwise, they'll attack one of my sick plants. Not one has escaped them to this point; the moment a plant is a little weak, they go after it mercilessly until it dies.

Sometimes I feel like my cats are my most faithful companions, but there are moments when I want to wring their necks.

Shakespeare, especially, doesn't seem to be scared of my murderous thoughts. I nicknamed her my Olympic cat because when she chases flies, she leaps to stunning heights. But she's also much too inquisitive. One day, she decided to explore the garbage can. I didn't think I needed to put a cover on it, because my cats were so well brought up. But a can of tomato sauce got rid of this veneer of civilization in a hurry. First with her face, then with her paws, Shakespeare scrupulously studied all the secrets of Catelli sauce. I didn't see her do it, of course; neither did Sylvain. But the paw prints on the upholstery left no doubt. After she had explored the garbage can, Shakespeare took a long stroll through the house.

For my birthday, Martin gave me a present that was very practical: a garbage can with a lid.

But Shakespeare had not exhausted her resources. The time she walked in the ashes of the fireplace before making her merry way throughout the apartment, she managed to involve Dali in her prank. Dear Shakespeare!

How did Sylvain resist the temptation to wring her neck? How did he manage not to banish her for life or take her to the SPCA? I have no idea. I only know that, like me, he simply grabbed a rag and cleaned up.

Sometimes, their little outrageous tricks weren't so funny. One day, worried because I hadn't arrived at the airport, Julie called our house. When she hung up, she was ten times more worried. Someone had answered, but she had heard only little stifled cries.

"Karine! Karine!" she shouted. "Are you there?"

She called back again and again, but the line was always busy.

In fact, I was on the highway, caught in a terrible traffic

jam. Ice and snow had caused an accident and there was complete gridlock. Meanwhile, the Ontario judges were waiting in Toronto for the Vilagos twins and me to show them our Olympic routines.

With fear in her heart, Julie finally decided to leave with Penny and Vicky. But what would the judges say? We had asked them to come and evaluate our routines, and the soloist wasn't even there.

Three flights later, I finally arrived in Toronto. Hungry and exhausted, my nerves in a knot, I dived in. The comments were positive, fortunately. This was the only good news of the day.

Julie was still curious. What in the devil had answered my phone?

When I got home, the phone was off the hook. What could have happened? It was only later that I figured it out. When the telephone rang, Picasso ran and took the receiver off the hook with her paw. Whether she liked the sound, was curious or exasperated, I'll never know. The judges' comments were encouraging, that was the important thing.

Everything was rolling right along. Karine had become a true champion. After the World Cup, the competitions piled up and so did the victories. Bonn, with Beethoven and the trip into the jungle; Liechtenstein; Brno, Czechoslovakia; Germany; Japan; Rome . . . Every trip involved its own adventure.

When I left for Brno in November 1991, I wasn't in top form; I felt weak and out of shape. In the abbey where the Vilagos, Julie, and I were staying, I slept sitting up, a glass of water beside me on the night table. But this didn't keep me from taking advantage of the trip to get to know the very friendly Czech people.

Since I spoke a bit of German, the cook, a charming white-haired man, took us under his wing. Every time we came back with a fresh victory, he brought out a bottle of champagne. I won the figures, the preliminaries, then the final in solo, and the twins did the same in duet. And the corks kept popping.

"Cheers!"

We drank a lot, but I didn't bounce back quite as fast as I would have wished. All the same, since we were much stronger than our adversaries, our celebrations didn't threaten our performances and so we didn't deprive ourselves. For once, we could let ourselves go a little.

"Cheers!"

My mind, already lulled by the warm welcome, the beauty of the country, and the cook's enthusiasm, asked only for tranquillity. My excuse was always that alcohol relaxes one. Perhaps I would finally be able to get to sleep.

It was only when I got home that I found out I had bronchitis.

When the Japanese issued an invitation to Julie and me, we were a little hesitant. With the Olympics just a few months away, it was risky to venture to the country of one of our main competitors. The Japanese soloist, a tiny girl barely a metre and a half tall, was surprisingly powerful, full of energy, and very fast.

At the pool, we were a couple of foreigners awash in a sea of a hundred and fifty Japanese girls. The panel was even worse: not a single foreign judge, only Japanese. What kind of hornet's nest had we stepped into? On top of that, I had this damned cut on my bikini line that kept bleeding.

After the preliminaries, the two Japanese girls were in the lead. It was only in the final that I managed to get ahead.

I would see the Japanese girls again in Rome a month later. I hadn't lost any of the competitiveness I had tested in Tokyo. Bring on the Japanese!

Rome was my last competition before the Games.

Until then, we had kept the Olympic routine carefully under wraps. From time to time, I would perform it for the

Canadian judges or for a chosen few, to test it and to know if it was good enough. On those days, we scrutinized faces. There were never many people at the pool, but if there was someone we didn't know, we checked his or her identity.

We had our spies at every competition in the United States and Western Canada; obviously, our adversaries were doing the same thing. So we couldn't give the slightest hint of what we were doing. In official competition, I swam my world championship routine, while I slaved away at my Vangelis music in training.

But the Olympics were just around the corner. It was time to unveil the new program; if we had to make adjustments, now was the time to find out.

Good God! It wasn't possible! In position on the edge of the pool, I suddenly knew that something wasn't right. The music was too fast, much too fast . . .

There was no question of complaining. Once the music begins, a swimmer has only one opportunity to swim, and she has to do her best.

I swam. When I came to the surface, I didn't have the time to take the breath I'd planned before diving back under again. As for the Vangelis, it sounded like a sound track for a cartoon.

I would have liked to give up. I was dying.

When it was finally over, the Italians apologized, saying that the cassette had taken eleven seconds less than it was supposed to. What a difference eleven seconds can make. Then they kindly offered me the chance to start again.

"Are you crazy?" I retorted. "Do you want to kill me?"

At any rate, my performance was good enough to assure me the victory.

Why, then, when I left Rome with the gold medal around my neck, did I write in my diary, "Goodbye, Rome. Who knows, maybe it's the last time in my life that I'll win a competition . . ."

Up till then, the prospect of the Olympics hadn't bothered me too much. Karine was immensely self-confident, she
was world champion, unbeaten in three years, so what could
happen to her? And what could happen to me?

In Rome, I realized that, in fact, lots of things could
happen. The runaway cassette had given me a good fright.
Yes, something horrible could happen to me, as it had happened to speed skater Sylvie Daigle, who only once in her
career had caught the blade of an adversary and fallen. It just
had to be at the Games. And look at Kurt Browning, world
champion from 1989 to 1991, who was injured and could do
no better than sixth place at the same Games. Thinking about
it, and I thought about it more and more, I was starting to get
worried. I imagined all the horror stories: serious injury, of
course, but also my tape twisting, music going too fast, as it
had in Rome, losing my nose plugs . . .

I replayed all these nightmares in my head ad nauseum,
awake or asleep. I thought of everything but what actually
happened.

But before that nightmare, there were still some wonderful dreams to come true.

THIRTEEN

Happy Birthday, Boubou

In recent years, I had never been able to celebrate my birthday with my family. There was always a competition or a training camp. Julie would take me out to dinner, and the girls would sing "Happy Birthday" around a small cake provided by the restaurant. This Olympic year would be no exception. It would be my twenty-fifth birthday — I'd be a quarter century old! — and on June 27, I would be in the hot sun, at a pool in Puerto Rico, working on my Olympic routine for Barcelona.

It was the end of May or the beginning of June, and I'd be leaving for Rome in a few days. Then, after a short three-day stopover at home, I would leave for Puerto Rico. We had just done a show at CAMO, the last before the Games. It was a Sunday, one of my last days off, and I intended to enjoy it. And Sylvain seemed to feel the same way: "Let's be lazy and stay in bed."

But I was hungry; a bowl of cereal would be nice. I was about to get up when Sylvain jumped out of bed: "I'll make you a little something." As he left the room, he closed the door that overlooked the downstairs.

He was acting a little strange. But it was so hot and I felt so relaxed stretched out on the bed. The tinny sound of the radio, which Sylvain had turned up just about full, was getting on my nerves, but I was too lazy to move. So, to heck with the radio!

"I put the cats away so they'll calm down. They're so excited," he told me when he came back.

My cats weren't bothering us, though. At least not that day . . .

"You can be so impatient with them, Sylvain. What will you do while I'm away?"

We felt good, lying in bed, doing nothing. Suddenly, I heard a strange noise, like a paper bag being crumpled. It was nothing, I thought at first, just one of the cats. But no, Sylvain had put them in the garage.

"Sylvain, there's someone in the house. It's a robber."

Without thinking, I got up and ran down the stairs, with Sylvain, barechested, at my heels — and then I saw them. There were thirty or forty people gathered in the apartment, and they had just finishing hanging balloons and streamers. Everyone was there: the Fréchettes, the Charbonneaus, and Sylvain's entire family.

"Happy birthday, Boubou!"

Aunt Nicole had come up with the idea: before I left, why not throw me a surprise party? The timing was right; my birthday was coming up. When Sylvain suggested a date, Aunt Nicole organized everything. But Sylvain had a most delicate task: to keep me busy so that I wouldn't suspect anything. This wasn't too difficult a job for him. He always liked organizing things and people. Usually, as on that day, while I was looking at the banner and the balloons, I loved this quality. But at other times, I had to grit my teeth a little.

For example, there was the story of Mom and the video tape. She had always told him, "Sylvain, don't ever tape me."

For some time, Sylvain had been directing a series of film clips on Olympic hopefuls. These clips were usually broadcast as part of the news. For mine, he had more room to manoeuvre; since the program was sponsored, he had all of thirty minutes to talk about me. Of course, he wanted the film on me to be the best, the most thorough, the most touching — and he had a lot of material to work with. My mother had supplied him with old home movies of me as a child, playing in the bath and even being held by my father.

Now, he wanted Mom to be one of the stars of the film, but she refused. Far from being discouraged, he was more determined than ever to get his way. Mom had always been and still was so important to me that I too wanted her to be in the film. So I agreed to work with him.

Stretched out on Mom's bed, I interviewed her. Sylvain pretended to be testing the camera. As she stroked my hair in her usual way, she answered my questions in a soft voice, breathing her confidences in a whisper.

"Will it bother you when I retire?"

"I can't wait. Finally, you'll be able to live . . ."

Poor Mom. When she finally realized that she had been manipulated, she felt betrayed. Her disappointment hurt me. But when she saw the results, she was proud. If she had been aware that the camera was on, she might not have been as good, and she knew it. But she still had a little twinge in her heart.

Sylvain's initiatives often provoked these ambivalent reactions. Dear Sylvain, so adorable and yet so exasperating.

One morning, he came home wearing the grin of a guy who had just slipped one over on someone . . .

"Have you read the paper today?"

No, I hadn't read it yet.

In it was an article about Sylvain's transition from sports to politics, since he was running for city councillor in Hochelaga-Maisonneuve.

"Wow! Sylvain, that's wonderful!"

Suddenly, I caught my breath. It couldn't be. No, not

this! In the paper, he was announcing to all the world that he was madly in love and that he wanted to marry me.

"Sylvain," I gasped, "how many people read this before I did?"

I never imagined a marriage proposal coming like this. Although I was smiling, part of me was grimacing — the real Sylvie, timid, reserved, who would have liked to keep her relationship a secret, hide it away like a treasure, while Sylvain wanted to shout it from the rooftops. But, this, truly, was the last straw. I wanted his proposal to be romantic, wrapped in gauzy cotton, not in newsprint . . .

One little part of me wanted to shout, Hurray! But the other part retorted, Hell, no! Sylvain, this really isn't right. How can you do something like this?

In the end, we did get engaged, and we even set a date for our wedding in September 1991. My dress was chosen, the guest list written. We didn't want flowers; we thought balloons would be more fun. Marie-Denise Pelletier, the daughter of a Rosemont neighbour, a dear friend of my Grandmother Fréchette, was to sing at our ceremony. She and I had seen each other at a *La Presse* gala, and we were immediately drawn to each other.

But the pressures were mounting. There was the World Cup in Bonn, and the wedding would be practically the day I got home. Coming up later, but not that far in the future, were the Olympics. I looked at my schedule and immediately burst into tears. How would everything get done in time? I couldn't sleep; I felt like I was suffocating, and I wasn't even in the water.

A pre-Olympic competition, scheduled at the last minute, was the final blow to our folly. Logic prevailed. It would be better to wait until after the Games, where Sylvain would be a commentator and I an athlete. Anyway, we wouldn't have had the time to have a honeymoon. And besides, we would have our entire lives to love each other.

We chose a new date: June 26, 1993.

But on the day of the surprise party, nothing could spoil my good mood. For me, there had never been anything like this party with my family. It was just marvellous. What a wonderful idea! Only my family could have thought of it.

My uncle made a touching speech. The Charbonneaus, who always cried at the drop of a hat, dabbed at their eyes. The magic of the cottage, and all the happiness that we had felt when we were together there, seemed to have been transported to our apartment.

Games were organized, and there was even a putting contest in the middle of the living room. Those who got a hole in one won a t-shirt. Throughout my childhood, my mother had organized games for the neighbourhood kids, giving a prize hat, bolo, or yoyo to the winner. For my friends, a visit to our home was like a trip to the carnival. For the surprise party, the principle was the same, but the prizes had changed a little. Sometimes, the winner even received a big prize: a Brita jug.

Brita . . . I must say that as my agent, Sylvain was not idle. He took care of my agenda, which included the difficult assignment of turning down certain invitations. I was incapable of doing this; if someone pushed just a little, I gave in. God knows how I would manage to be in three places at once.

He had also gotten me a few sponsors. In at least one case, the task was easy. "Sylvie, I got a call from National, the public relations firm," he told me. "Someone wants to sponsor you."

This was in 1991, a little after the article on the poor, penniless champion and, since the incident with the dry cleaner, I was a bit mistrustful. As well, like almost all Quebecers, the name "Brita" didn't mean a thing to me, and I didn't want to be associated with just any product.

But the money was tempting. It wouldn't hurt to meet with Daniel Lamarre at National. Lamarre, who had thought of me, was responsible for the Brita account. After meeting him, Sylvain said, "O.K., he's fine." It remained to be seen what we thought of Brita.

I reviewed the situation. The product, a water filter, had a good reputation. The annual income would enable me to pay off my debts. I owed money to everyone, including Mom, and Sylvain sometimes had to pay our entire rent. My car, an old, accident-scarred jalopy that I had bought for a song, no longer worked, and I didn't even have money to pay the young man who gave me a discount on repairs.

I met with Mr. Moss Kadey, the president of Brita. "I need someone to get the ball rolling in Quebec," he told me. "My product isn't known here."

I liked him right away. He was straightforward and had the right values.

"I want you to get to the Games," he continued. "If you need anything . . ."

I paid off my debts and had some money left over. On my birthday, Mr. Kadey always sent me a card and flowers. He never asked for more than five days per year of my time. I think that, in a way, I was his charity case.

That was the happy side of the champion's life. But there were also some disagreeable parts, such as the time when a journalist, surprised not to see me at a press conference, gave me a good going-over in an article. Now that I was a world champion, he wrote, I shunned press conferences, and I was too big for my britches. When I read this, I was furious. I had been informed of the press conference at the last minute, I had a training session, and, at the very same time, I had another interview — with a journalist from his own newspaper. He later apologized, but I never again talked to him as openly.

But I've strayed far from the subject at hand — my birthday. At the surprise party, Sylvain decided to give out Brita jugs as first prizes.

Only Grandfather was missing. It's strange: even today, I can sense his presence, as if he's so close that I can touch him. I know that I'm not the only one to have this feeling. It's impossible to go into any house in the Charbonneau family without seeing a picture of Grandpa and my cousin Jean-François, and they'll always be with me.

Yes, Grandpa would have liked this day. The best thing about it was the generosity of all these people who'd come to celebrate and wish me good luck. They brought everything: the food, the dishes, the cutlery, the tables, the chairs. And they took everything away with them, leaving our apartment as clean as a whistle, as if nothing had happened there.

If only I'd known how much I would need them soon . . .

*

FOURTEEN

No!

Saturday, July 18, 1992. We were in a hurry that morning. We had been in a hurry for some time, but that day, it was worse. Sylvain was leaving for Barcelona in the evening. As for me, I hadn't slept well and I was tense. I had to present my routine to the Canadian judge assigned to the Games, which made me nervous. Then, after training and bodybuilding, I had a photo session for the *Gazette*. Happily, Sylvain and I had had some quiet time together the previous day.

When I came back from the introduction of the Olympic team in Toronto on Friday afternoon, we decided to treat ourselves to an intimate dinner out. It would be our last before the Games, for soon we'd really be on the run. And all this rushing around would only plunge us more deeply into the Olympic whirlpool. We were already hyped up and tense. For me, the Olympic Games represented the culmination of eighteen years of work. I was anxious, and I imagine that Sylvain, who would have liked to experience the Olympics as an athlete but was going as a commentator, also had a tight throat. These Games were *our* Games. One more great effort to give, fifteen days of craziness, no doubt the most exciting and tiring two weeks of our lives, and then we could finally live like a normal couple.

When he got up Saturday morning, Sylvain didn't seem to be himself. Ever since I'd known him, every once in a while, he had moments of total inertia, as if he suddenly shifted into neutral. He would stare at the ceiling or the walls, completely indifferent to what was going on around him. He'd blank out out, literally, for hours, sometimes even days. When he came out of it, he was always more energetic than ever and more than ready to move mountains. I think that, just like listening to music always unknotted my muscles, it was his way of relaxing.

On my way out, I said to him, "I'll try to be fast. I'll see you this afternoon. We'll talk a little before I take you to the airport." When he didn't answer, it didn't really surprise me.

I wasn't at all in the mood for training or the photo session or the running from one place to the next at full speed. I was tired and I just wanted to get it over with and get home to share a few quiet minutes with Sylvain before he left. I speeded up the photo session as much as I could. Finally, it was over, and I went home.

As I opened the door, the smell caught at my nose and throat.

Sylvain!

The car engine was running. Sylvain was in the garage. I had to find him. Oh, my God! Sylvain, no!

The smell coming out of the exhaust pipe was absolutely disgusting. But Sylvain wasn't in the car. It didn't occur to me to turn the car off before I ran upstairs.

"Sylvain, where are you?"

Crying and trembling, I ran upstairs in utter panic. I checked the first floor, then the second. The smell was making my heart jump, and I could barely keep from vomiting. Quick, quick!

I finally found him, all the way upstairs. He was lying on

the bed, his feet on the pillow and his head at the foot of the bed. His arms were dangling over the edge.

"Sylvain! Sylvain, wake up!"

His too-white back was covered with large black and blue splotches. His face was lying in the liquid that had flowed from his mouth.

There was no response, no reaction.

"Sylvain, answer me!"

I went to shake him, and then I had the shock of my life. His skin was so cold . . . Suddenly, everything seemed so unreal. I didn't understand right away. But I knew I needed help. An emergency. I had to dial 911.

But there were all these questions. My name, my address, who was hurt . . . I was furious with the operator for taking so much time. What are you waiting for? Help us!

She finally got a doctor on the line.

I hadn't even thought of opening a window before I called. The emergency doctor didn't think of it either. "Turn him over," he repeated again and again. "Try to take his pulse."

His pulse! Without knowing why, I found the doctor horribly stupid and I began to swear — I who had never sworn in my life. If he had been there, I would have slapped him. Take his pulse! But it was ridiculous. What I had touched was no longer alive.

It was then that I understood. I think I screamed, "His pulse? But he's blue and stiff. Don't you get it? He's dead! He's dead!"

He insisted: "Try to revive him!"

"But I can't even turn him over. I can't, I can't . . ."

When I came to, I was lying on the grass in front of the house. The ambulances and police were there.

Later, someone explained to me that I was in a state of shock, that the 911 operators had done what they could to keep me on the telephone. But at that moment, I found everyone so stupid, so useless.

A neighbour came running: "Is he dead? Is he dead?"
I hit her.

Inside, the police and paramedics were busy. I ran in.

"Don't touch that. Those are *our* things. Those are *his* things."

I didn't want to answer all their questions. "I just want to be with him. Let go of me. Don't touch me!"

These details come back to me in flashes in the middle of my nightmares. In Barcelona, people performed verbal contortions to avoid talking to me about it. If only they knew. I can't stop thinking about it. Night and day, asleep and awake, I live through the same nightmare. Will I finally wake up someday?

I watched all the police officers and paramedics rushing around my house. "So, do something!"

It was too late, and I knew it. Softly, a police officer suggested, "Can you call someone?"

Mom! That day, she was at Jean-Pierre's. Fortunately, he was the one who answered.

"Don't ask any questions. Come over right away with Mom."

Outside, the police had blocked off the street. The neighbours had already gathered in front of the house. Most of them were much older than Sylvain and me, and they saw us as the young lovebirds, the model couple. They didn't understand, either. How could such a thing have happened? Sylvain, why? *Why?*

If only I hadn't gone out that morning . . . but why wouldn't I have gone out?

It was my fault, I should have known . . .

Mom! She wouldn't be able to get past the police, who were stopping everyone . . . I stood by the window. Mom had to get through. Somehow, I had to get her through. I tried to concentrate on this thought, but in vain.

The Lakes! Someone had to tell them about their son.

How do you tell people that their son is dead? How could I tell them that I had done nothing to keep him from taking his own life?

I called his sister, Josée. She was strong, she'd be able to talk to them . . .

Apparently, I also called Julie, but I don't remember. There are still a lot of holes in my memory.

So that he wouldn't take the cats with him, Sylvain had put them out on the balcony. He had even made a canvas shelter on the patio table to protect them from the rain. Sylvain! I knew that you loved my cats! He had put my world-championship ring from 1986, which I had always found too heavy and which he had agreed to wear, on the night table. When I gave it to him, I said to myself, "He has been an athlete, too. He'll understand that I'm offering him a part of myself." He had never taken it off.

Even today, I don't know exactly the order in which things happened. In some cases, I don't even know if I remember them myself or if someone told me about them. All that I remember for sure is my feeling of horror and despair. I saw the stretcher roll out, leaving two parallel lines on the carpet, and it's as if those two lines trapped me forever in my nightmare.

"Mom, get me out of here!"

Soon, the journalists arrived. They wanted to know what had happened, wanted me to tell them.

Mom took me to Jean-Pierre's. No one except our immediate family knew that Jean-Pierre existed. For the moment, it was the ideal retreat.

But first of all, I absolutely had to talk to the Lakes. Mr. Lake and Reggie, Josée's husband, had come to the apartment, but all the others — his mother, his sister, his brother, Jocelyn — stayed home. I wanted to see them. Jean-Pierre had brought two of the cats. Mom and I took the other two and went over in my car. Since Mom didn't know how to drive a standard, I had to drive. In my state, it was completely crazy.

A terrible silence reigned at the Lakes'. They had already gone through the initial shock with the phone call. Now there was just a terrible despair that might have passed, at first glance, for calm. Literally crushed, they had trouble saying anything.

In my family, the news spread quickly. When we arrived at Jean-Pierre's, everyone was there.

Martin! Until then, I hadn't realized how big and strong my little brother had gotten. His arms wrapped around me as he told me, "I'll always be there for you."

Grandma had come in from the country. She didn't say anything, but it was all in her eyes. I knew she understood, since she, too, had found her man dead. In fact, of everyone there who was crying with me, she was perhaps the only one who knew exactly what thoughts were tumbling around in my head.

"It's my fault. If only I'd stayed with him . . . Why did it happen? Why this? Why now? I'd like to rip your guts out, Sylvain Lake. How could you do this to us? How could you do it to me, me? I love you . . . It's my fault, my fault . . .

Above all was a terrible feeling of guilt, a feeling that I could have changed fate if only I had done something different.

I've heard that Sylvain's mother explained her son's death this way: "Sylvain suffered from the pain of living." This is no doubt the most reasonable explanation I've heard for Sylvain's decision.

At Jean-Pierre's, newspapers were piling up, but I refused to read them. I didn't want to know what they were saying, but I wanted them to be kept; I would read them later, after the Games. So, I didn't know that, a few hours after his death, milllions of strangers who didn't know him learned that he had tried to kill himself a number of years before. Oh, Sylvain! Who told them? Who?

Sylvain would not have wanted people to know, I'm very sure. As for me, far from making me feel better, this information made me feel even more guilty. I should have guessed. I should have known how much he was suffering, warded off the worst . . . Instead, I had simply believed that he was fine with me, that my presence alone was enough for him, that our little differences amounted to nothing compared with the strength of our love. How pretentious!

I felt like Sylvain had taken me with him; I even kept smelling the revolting stench from the exhaust pipe. I watched the most insipid television programs, trying, in vain, to push the nightmare away. But even right in the middle of a rerun of an American golf tournament, between the eighth and ninth holes, it came to haunt me: "We interrupt this program to announce that Sylvain Lake, the companion of synchronized swimming champion Sylvie Fréchette . . ."

I wanted to surround myself with people whom I love and who love me, to protect me, to make a sort of cocoon in which I could hide. My family, Sylvain's, Julie, the other synchronized swimmers . . . Having lots of people around kept me from thinking.

Like many others, Nathalie Audet came to see me. I had called her at 6:30 Sunday morning; I didn't want her to find out about Sylvain from the newspapers. Later, she told me what had happened when she visited me. During her pregnancy, she used to come over to show off her growing belly. She and I always had something to talk about besides synchronized swimming; often, we talked about Sylvain. By now, Nathalie had had her baby, but between competitions, training, and interviews, I hadn't yet had the time to see her son.

Nathalie came to Jean-Pierre's with her husband, Donald, and the baby. She didn't really know what to say. Donald took the baby and put him in my arms. I just went "Ahhh," and the world suddenly began to make sense again. The ice was broken.

I don't remember this episode. I'm sure that there are still a lot of holes in my memory, but I'm not sure that I really want to fill them in.

I was a little uncomfortable; poor Jean-Pierre was being invaded by my family, my friends, and my cats — and he was allergic to cats . . . Later that Sunday morning, I also called Luc. He had helped me when I had missed the 1988 Games. He was more than a sports psychologist, he was also a friend. As gentle as ever, he asked me, "What are you going to do about the Games?"

"Games? What Games?"

"The Olympic Games."

"What Olympic Games?"

Wrapped up in my pain, plunged into my nightmare, I had completely forgotten the Olympics. I had forgotten that I wasn't only Sylvie, but also Karine.

What was I going to do?

Karine kicked me in the behind: "Wake up, my girl. There's nothing left *but* the Games. You'll cry afterward. You'll have your whole life for that."

While my family was pampering me, the pressure of synchronized swimming was pushing me. Julie wanted to see me in the pool Monday morning. It wasn't indifference, or even cynicism. She knew that only swimming could save me. There was nothing else. My fiancé had died, and with him, our entire future as a couple. I no longer had an apartment, since I could never live in that unhappy place. No car anymore, either.

"Damned car! Sell it, give it away, I never want to see it again," I told Martin.

We would never make the trips we had dreamed about. I would never have the children we had wanted . . . My future had died with Sylvain. If I didn't go to the Games, I would also have to mourn for eighteen years of my life. Julie knew that.

Mr. Lake also brought me back to reality, as he had done once before at the apartment. He kept telling me, "It was his own choice. It isn't your fault. You're alive. You have a job to do, and you must do it."

These Games weren't just my Games, they were our Games, Sylvain's and mine. They had been our dream. If I could save even a part of them, I had to do it.

On Monday, I was in the pool. I went at 6:30 a.m., to avoid the reporters who wanted to talk to me, to see how I was doing . . . In spite of this, a photographer somehow managed to get in, but he was pushed back out the door before he could get to me. I didn't want to meet the journalists: "All they want is dirt. Let them leave me in peace. I'll talk to them after the Games. Now, I just want to swim."

I barely remember that either . . .

I do remember, however, that in the water, and only there, I was free from my pain and suffering. I entered another world, my own universe, and Karine's. Only there did I manage to forget. Only there did I turn back into Karine.

The first day, all I did was get wet; fifty-five minutes isn't really a training session. But once I was in the water, I felt a little like I was being reborn.

Gradually, I started training again. Mom came to the pool, and so did Pascale, Martin's long-time girlfriend, almost my sister-in-law. In the days before I left for the Games, she became the sister I'd never had. I'd always thought highly of her: she was a strong, healthy girl, not complicated, and as calm as Martin could be impetuous.

Mom wanted to sleep with me, to console me and stroke my hair, but she was suffering from a terrible cold. Since I wasn't eating or sleeping, a cold would have finished me off. Although she didn't say so, she also probably thought that I needed a companion my own age, a confidante. It must have broken her heart, but she yielded the place that would normally have been hers. So it was Pascale who slept with me. In fact, we didn't sleep much; instead, we talked, about everything and nothing. About Sylvain, too. I tried to concentrate on the good times. But most of the time, I cried, and Pascale cried with me.

She and Mom came to the pool with me. Their presence both comforted me and reminded me of Sylvain. Often, I caught them crying, and I began to cry, too. Natou, Annie, and Nathalie came as well. I knew that they would never drag themselves out at dawn to watch me swim. They were there because Sylvain wasn't anymore . . .

When I wasn't crying or swimming, I shut myself up in my own world. Some pretty strange things happened there, to judge by some of things I did.

It was Annie who told me about this, but I must admit that I haven't the slightest memory of it, and I have trouble believing that it happened. I was coming back from the weight room. I had put my hair up in a ponytail and I was skipping from foot to foot like a little girl going to school, swinging my ponytail from one side to the other. Oh, my God! What could have been going on in my head? Nathalie and Annie looked at each other anxiously, sure that I was losing my mind. Perhaps they were right.

"Make Ms. Fréchette eat her pasta. She's getting thin and she's losing her strength. Make her eat."

In fact, I was a shadow of myself. So where was Karine?

To keep things going, to get through my routine, I would have to outdo myself, or almost . . . I called Luc Pelletier, again and again, every evening until I left.

My Olympic routine was pure folly, at the limits of human capacity. It was three and a half minutes of torture, including two minutes and ten seconds with my head underwater. The first figure was forty-two seconds without a breath. We must have been completely nuts to dream up something like that. At first, I couldn't even execute all of my first figure, and I couldn't raise myself higher than my knees.

"Julie, we're out of our minds. Have you thought of that? In skating, if you can't do it, you fall on your bum, but in synchro, as you know, you pass out."

Through training and bodybuilding, I had achieved near perfection, and I knew it. Now, with the Games a few days away, I had completely lost my strength. I couldn't complete even a third of the routine. Taking stock of the damage, Julie was utterly distressed and discouraged, but she didn't reveal this to me. All the same, there was no question of letting the journalists in. Although they weren't very well informed about synchronized swimming, my pitiful condition would have been all too obvious to them. They mustn't know. No one must know.

But I wasn't aware of this. All I knew was that I felt all right in the water. If I had known more, I no doubt would have stayed home, under the covers, crying my eyes out. I wanted so much to be able to cry in peace . . .

I don't think I realized to what point we were skirting disaster until we got to Barcelona. The fact that my first training sessions in Spain had to be conducted in two parts because I wasn't capable of performing the routine from beginning to end hadn't particularly hit me. I was in an altered state; I was barely surviving, and it had not occurred to me to ask myself questions. On my second day in Barcelona, however, when I managed to get through my routine without crying for mercy, I understood. Never, ever, had I been so scared.

The journalists took their places in the stands. Julie looked at me and said, "Today, you'll do the whole thing."

And I couldn't . . . And it was so bad that even the most ignorant journalists could see it.

But it was their presence that gave me the little push I

needed. My two arms in the air as if it was the greatest victory in my life, I finished my program. My smile went from ear to ear. It hadn't been perfect, but at least I'd done the whole thing. Finally! During the competition, with the extra adrenalin, everything would go better. I could afford to feel a little self-confident once more. But it was only now, performing for journalists who were worried that I would crack, that I realized that I could very well not have made it. Any little thing could have pushed me over the edge. If the synchronized-swimming competition had been scheduled at the beginning of the Games rather than the end, for example, it would have been over for me!

In my little bubble in the Georges-Vernot pool, I didn't worry about anything, leaving all the worries to Julie: keeping the journalists at bay, giving me a bit of strength, answering the questions . . .

From time to time, though, Karine resurfaced. In fact, she struck Mom one of the worst blows she had ever received. Since Sylvain's death, Mom had pampered me, cried with me, felt sorry for me.

"If you don't want to swim, my dear," she told me, "you don't have to . . ."

I exploded: "I need to do it. And I need strong people around me. If all you can do is cry, I'd rather you not be here. I don't need that . . ."

Seeing her devastated face, I softened a little: "Mom, try to understand. I have to go to the Games. That's all that's left for me. That's all I know how to do . . ."

No one wanted me to go to the morgue. But I insisted. People couldn't understand. I didn't want to keep the memory of the Sylvain I'd seen in the apartment. Right after training on Tuesday, we went. Mom was there, with Pascale and Mr. and Mrs. Lake. Mr. Asselin, a Quebec Police Force officer and an old neighbour who had come to console me after the 1988 Olympics, came with us. As soon as I saw

Sylvain's face, I knew I was right to come. There was nothing contorted about his face anymore. Never had I seen him so relaxed; he looked just like he was sleeping. At any rate, death had never scared him. He saw it as an adventure. Now, finally, he looked happy, peaceful. I was happy there, with my handsome lover who was smiling in his sleep. I could have stayed there forever . . . When they began to close the curtain, I rebelled: "I don't want to go right away."

I was leaving for Barcelona the next day. I knew that I would never see him again. They had to drag me away. In the elevator, Mr. Asselin and Mom held me up. But when the doors opened at the ground floor, I lost my head.

In the QPF building, the radio was playing "Petite Marie," by Francis Cabrel. At the beginning of our relationship, this song was very popular, and Sylvain would sing it to me as "Petite Sylvie."

"I come from heaven and the stars talk about you . . ."

"Mom, it's him. He's talking to me!" I was not in my right mind. "It's him, Mom, I know it." I became hysterical and I was as limp as a rag doll when they got me into the car.

On the way home, we stopped off at the doctor's. I was terribly sick to my stomach.

The doctor weighed me, took my blood pressure, and when he held out some medication, I was barely civil: "I don't want your pills."

However, I swallowed them. After a few minutes, he looked me in the eye and asked me, "How do you feel now?"

The pain had gone completely.

"My dear," he told me, "you have an ulcer."

The next day, Wednesday, I was scheduled to fly to Barcelona.

I hesitated. Sylvain's funeral wasn't taking place until Saturday, the day of the opening ceremonies. I wanted everything to happen as he would have wished. He had always hated long sermons, and he would have wanted a very simple service.

In spite of everything, I decided to go to Barcelona. But before getting on the plane, I had to face a last trial. Until then, I had held off the journalists: "Wait until I'm ready." Now, it was time, and I knew it. I'd had my differences with them, and their lack of knowledge of my sport sometimes frustrated me, but on the whole they had supported me and I thought of them as friends. I owed them this much. So, just before my flight, Julie organized a press conference at Dorval Airport.

I asked my family to be there, and everyone who wasn't working came. Mr. and Mrs. Lake were there, too. I had managed to put on a more or less normal face; I could even dredge up a weak smile. But when it was time to go in, when I saw the cameras, when I saw neighbours and friends mixed in with the reporters, I panicked. I backed up, feeling faint, and they had to walk me to a nearby room.

"I can't go in there. I can't do it."

Julie talked to me, as she always had talked to Karine, simply and persuasively. "Be strong," she said. "Say what you have to say. That's all. No one is asking more."

I finally went in by a side door. All I remember are some vague impressions. Mom playing with my hair. Martin standing like a pillar behind me. The churchlike silence while I was speaking, then the applause when I stood to leave. I know that at one point I cried. At the end, I felt immense relief. Not just because I had managed to accomplish something that I thought I wasn't strong enough to do, but also because, as I had requested, everyone was satisfied with my statement and no one asked any questions.

I found out what I'd said when I read the newspapers: "No one is in a position to judge the situation or to ask questions. Myself, I don't have any answers, and I will continue to wonder for a long time. We must respect his choice. If you say hurtful things, I'm the one you'll be hurting.

"I have trained for eighteen years to give the best of myself in the Olympics. Synchronized swimming is in my blood. Those who knew Sylvain know what the Olympic Games meant to both of us. I will be swimming there with my own heart and Sylvain's . . ."

I finally boarded the plane with Julie and the Vilagos sisters. Sylvain had decided to stay in Montreal. In the plane, my heart was tight. How would people react over there, in Barcelona?

FIFTEEN

Barcelona

I had my first real test during the stopover in Toronto. The Canadian judo team was also on its way to Barcelona. One of the members, Jean-Pierre Cantin, looked at me strangely. *No, it's not my imagination. He was looking at me as if I were a bizarre creature, I'm sure of it. Oh, my God! Will I have to suffer like this for the entire Games?*

I was right. But when I realized why he was giving me this look, I smiled, and my shoulders, which had risen a good five centimetres with nervousness, relaxed. Jean-Pierre had come directly from Japan and was heading for Barcelona without stopping in Montreal. He'd had no news from Quebec, and he didn't know what had happened. Poor Jean-Pierre! In his blissful ignorance, he was simply wondering why I hadn't said hello.

I couldn't help smiling. What a fool I was to think that the whole world revolved around me!

In Barcelona, the accreditation procedure, which usually dragged on, took only ten minutes. I found out later that I got special treatment because of the circumstances.

The first Canadian athlete I saw was Mark Tewksbury,

who knew. He came right over and gave me a big hug, twirling me around.

"Oh, Sylvie!" was all he said. This warm spontaneity literally melted my heart. What a nice man!

The ice was broken, and I felt like I could face everyone else. To dispel that inevitable awkward moment, to keep people from freezing, as they almost all did, I went up to them and said, "Hi, how are you?" And so we talked about sports and training. Sometimes, when someone mentioned it, I'd say, "Yes, my fiancé committed suicide. But I'm not here to listen to sermons. I'm here to swim and do my best, like everyone else."

For years, I had hoped to get to the Games, had imagined this moment, but it was nothing like I had dreamed it. Grandpa had died a few months before and would never again see me swim. And Grandma, my little Grandma, wanted so much to be there, but she had to stay behind in Montreal. For months, she had been sending entry forms in to a Brita contest offering tickets for the Games. She had asked the whole family to cut out forms from the newspapers for her, and she must have sent in fifty; all she won were three Brita jugs.

In our hearts, we were relieved. Since Grandpa had died, she had had high blood pressure, and an attack of angina had kept her from coming to greet me at the airport after the world championships. So none of us really wanted to see her, at the age of seventy-five, suffocating in the stifling heat of Barcelona.

Sylvain wasn't there either. He would never be there again.

For a year, in my diary, I had counted down the days left before the Games. Sometimes, I felt like a child waiting impatiently for Christmas. A few months before the Games, I had been invited to write a short column in the *Journal de Montréal*, a sort of personal journal. It seems strange to reread it. On April 17, I wrote, "I have the feeling that these 99 days will pass more slowly than the 18 years of training I've endured. In fact, I feel a bit like when I was a child at Christmas. I waited so impatiently for December 25. The 24th seemed to last for months."

And sometimes, in fact more and more often as the Games approached, I felt like a prisoner who was about to be released. I would have liked to escape, even for a moment, the ever-increasing pressure.

A few months before the Games, a man in his fifties came over to me in the produce section of the supermarket and said, "Bring us back the gold medal."

I wanted to run away. "Obviously, this gentleman was full of good intentions," I wrote in my May 1 column, "but I felt like he was giving me an order, as if someone were saying, 'Get me a glass of water.'"

That day, I reminded my readers that only three Quebecers had won gold at the Summer Games in ninety-six years, and then I told them that I was swimming for *me*, not for the medal.

I wanted the Games to take place immediately, right now. I saw them as a kind of deliverance for my body and soul. If only I'd known . . .

Now, I wish that time had stopped then, when Sylvain was still alive.

In Barcelona, I had to force myself not to think such futile thoughts. I didn't want to think about what I had just gone through, not yet. As soon as I arrived, I kept myself busy with the smallest details: "Oh, I'm going to brush my teeth." "Oh, I'll go eat. That will be good."

I tried to avoid my room, where my phantoms awaited me. Anyway, we were packed in so tight that if I rolled over I might hit Vicky, who was sleeping in the next bed; her sister was also sharing the room. I always felt a little uncomfortable sharing a room with the Vilagos twins; it was a bit like being along on someone's honeymoon. There were so few beds that Denise, one of our coaches, was sleeping on a massage table.

I preferred to take long, solitary walks with my Walkman in the Olympic Village. When I saw all the athletes in robes and turbans, I felt a little like Alice in Wonderland. I didn't dare speak to anyone; I was scared, and I knew that I was fragile.

In the airport, just before my flight, I had bought a horror novel, Stephen King's *Needful Things*. I wanted something ugly, twisted, and really repulsive, but especially a story in which I wouldn't recognize myself. I didn't want to read a love story or anything that would remind me of things I didn't want to think about, didn't want to remember. And it was in English, which would make me concentrate and keep my mind from wandering.

No one asked me indiscreet questions; even the journalists restrained themselves and asked only about my training. At the opening ceremonies, on July 25, they concentrated on one banal question, but one with lots of question marks after it: "How are you feeling today?"

In Barcelona, the Games were starting, but in Montreal, something was coming to an end. Sylvain was being buried. That night, my nightmare came back to haunt me.

The next day, in my diary, I didn't even know if my "Little Prince" still existed: "It seems that I'll have to rename you, I want to sell everything, change my wardrobe, my hair, my car . . . start all over again! Start over, but not forget. I have many things to remember, because I had good times. At the same time, there were darker periods . . . I can forget those, or at least soften them. I think I have to remember a bit, if I want to get past this. It won't be easy to go back home. It feels like I'll be going back to nothing: no more synchronized swimming, no more school. No more car, no more house, no more lover, no more best friend, no more Boubou. Never again . . . just in my head, just in my heart. "I'll stop here, because it makes me think too much and I had almost managed to forget." It's so difficult to think of nothing!

Sometimes, I read some of the letters that were pouring

July 1990: At the Swiss Open in Lancy, I won gold.
Here, I'm with Barbara Brenwald and Julie.

January 1991: A warm welcome from the CAMO club at Dorval airport
when I arrived home from the world championships.

January 1991: My brother, Martin, and me.

January 1991: My family was at Dorval to greet me, too.

May 1991: At the Canadian championships in Edmonton.

June 1991: The three solo winners at Roma Synchro.
Marjolain Both (Holland), 3rd; me, 1st; and Kristen Babb, 2nd.

June 1991: Performing at Roma Synchro.   1992: Sylvain and me.

August 1992: The three medallists at the Barcelona Olympic Games.
Kristen Babb-Sprague, me, and Fumiko Okuno.

ugust 1992: Arriving at Dorval from Barcelona: Martin, me, and Pascale.

September 1992: Olympic synchronized-swimming athletes and trainers at an Expos game at the Olympic Stadium. From left: Penny and Vicky Vilagos, Julie, Youppi, Andrzej Kuleska, and me.

January 1, 1993: the *Bye Bye* show!

in from Quebec. There were piles of mail every day, enormous helpings of encouragement and love that gave me my strength back. But occasionally there would be a hateful, aggressive letter, blaming me for Sylvain's death, and I would sink again, my heart heavier than ever. It was true, it was my fault. For this reason, Julie didn't want me to read my mail anymore. "You'll read all the letters afterward."

But it was stronger than me. The very day of the final, when I was in the middle of the computer error controversy, I received a new blow. "It's your fault!" the letter accused. "You're so egocentric, you were so wrapped up in yourself that you didn't even see he had problems . . ."

Oh, my God! How would I manage to swim?

But I'm getting ahead of myself, skipping steps. Let's go back a bit . . .

In training, I was having difficulty floating. I had gotten thinner, and my fat level wasn't high enough. So I got busy eating. One day, just before the preliminaries, I had four helpings of ice cream, one after the other. I love ice cream, almost as much as cheesecake. I can sure eat a lot when it's cheesecake! I had an enormous piece of cheesecake with a cappuccino when my participation in the Olympics was confirmed in Calgary, shortly before the Games.

The ice cream no doubt did the trick, because after the preliminaries on August 2, I found myself even with the American. It was a good sign, under the circumstances. Now that the preliminaries had sorted things out and identified the finalists, everything was erased and we started again at zero.

Julie, however, wasn't completely satisfied. "You swam well," she told me, "but not really with your guts. You swam safe."

I hadn't really noticed this at the time, but she was right. I'd always had this problem, although, for the last few years,

I had managed, through concentration, to overcome the block. How had it suddenly reappeared? Why? I knew it was important to impress the judges, to put my best foot forward, to project the image of a champion at all times . . .

The compulsories took place three days later.

The day before was Mom's birthday. I wrote in my diary in the privacy of my bed, "Happy birthday, Mom . . . forty-nine years old. As for me, I'm doing much better, in my head as well. I want it all to be over. The performance will take place in exactly forty-eight hours. I got a fax from everyone at RDS that made me cry. It's funny, I'm at a stage where little things like that make me cry."

I had always feared the compulsory figures. And now that I had a tendency to sink because I didn't have enough fat, I really wanted to get them over with.

The warm-up took place at six o'clock in the morning, under the moon and stars. It was ridiculous, since it was almost impossible for us to find our place in the pool in broad daylight. But it was the same problem, and the same anxiety, for all of us.

One figure in particular, the "crane," worried me. All the girls were scared of it. Since the body's entire weight is carried on the arms, it requires extraordinary physical strength to pull it off; there's no respite, and by the end, your arms feel like they're on fire. Before the Games, it had been one of my best figures, but now I wasn't strong enough . . . In fact, my legs trembled a bit, but I managed to complete it. When I saw the marks, I felt like God was on my side: they were excellent.

The "albatross," on the other hand, didn't scare me at all. Of course, when you spend a minute and a half underwater without breathing, you don't come out feeling fit as a fiddle. As usual, I felt a little dizzy, but it had gone well.

I didn't look at the marks. I could think of only one thing: "My girl, you're finished for life with compulsory figures." But I wasn't worried. "I've done my job. Now the judges have to do theirs."

Then a little alarm bell went off in my head, rousing me from my trance. Something was wrong. The marks were delayed. I looked toward the judges then turned to Julie: "They're discussing something. What's going on?"

The judges were getting more and more upset. One of them began to shout and gesticulate.

Finally, the marks came out: in the middle of all the 9s was a horrible 8.7.

We were completely in the dark. Something had happened, obviously, but what?

But the competition had already started again.

It was only later, by talking to various people, that Julie finally got the full picture: the Brazilian judge had pressed the wrong button, and when she realized it, she wanted to correct her mistake. But the computer stubbornly refused to register the change, despite her repeated attempts. So she began to shout.

"I wanted 9.7, not 8.7," she kept telling the assistant head judge, a Japanese woman who didn't understand a single word of her explanation.

Later, the Brazilian judge even said that my figure was the best she had seen that day. On the other hand, Kristen Babb said in an interview after the Games that the Brazilian probably hadn't recognized me, and that she had no doubt wanted to change her mark when she realized that she was dealing with the world champion. How she could have said such things, I'll never understand. She wasn't hurting just me, but our entire sport; her victories as well as mine could lose all their credibility . . . But that's another story.

The chief referee, an American, then came forward, and in the pandemonium, she ordered, over the Brazilian's protestations, that all discussion stop and that the marks be

posted at once. Then, she definitively put an end to my hopes:
"Let the competition continue!"

I began to panic. "Will the error be corrected?" Julie ran
around from one person to the next. As soon as I could get
near her, I bugged her constantly. In the meantime, Denise
and I did the calculations. Her hand was trembling. We
calculated the totals six times, but we were so rattled that we
didn't get the same result twice. Just one thing was sure. If
the 8.7 stood, I would lose the compulsories.

I began to cry. "But why is this happening to me?"

In another corner, the Brazilian judge was also weeping
bitterly.

At that moment, I ran into one of the Brazilian swimmers. "It's terrible what's happening to you, Sylvie," she said.

I was still stunned. "But, look, the judge has admitted her
error," I said. "Why can't she correct her mark?"

"She's my mother," the athlete answered, a sad look on
her face. "Come with me and we'll talk to her."

When she saw me, the Brazilian judge burst into tears.
"I didn't want to hurt you," she said. "I didn't do it on
purpose."

"Madam," I told her, "you have eighteen years of my life
in your hands. Promise me you'll do everything possible to
get justice."

In spite of all the hysteria and confusion, everyone was
sure that things would be worked out. It was so ridiculous, so
obvious an error that it would quickly be corrected.

We had half an hour to register a protest. At the time, I
didn't notice, but Kristen Babb came over to congratulate
me. I thanked her.

When I found out that the protest had been rejected, I
burst into tears: "Why is this still happening to me?" Between
sobs, I tried to talk to Julie. "Julie, what will you do? You have
to do something . . ."

Instead of being in first place, I was in fourth. The

margin was small, but almost insurmountable in a competition like the Olympic Games. To win the gold medal under these circumstances, Babb would have to sink like a stone and I would have to walk on water.

We appealed. We would not know the result until the next day, one hour before the solo final. How could I hope to stay motivated?

Convinced that the compulsories wouldn't hold any surprises at all, the journalists hadn't even attended. When they arrived right in the middle of the mess, they ran around like crazy gathering all the details of the story.

When I left the pool, Mom and Jean-Pierre were waiting for me. I fell, crying, into Mom's arms.

"What more can happen to me? Will I be run over by a bus? Let it come, I'm ready!"

Mom didn't understand anything, and I didn't know much more than she did. Hoping to cheer ourselves up, we went for a walk and tried to take some snapshots.

In the bus that took us back to the Olympic Village, I was still on the verge of tears, when from deep within me, Karine suddenly popped up. "My poor girl, that's exactly what they want, to demoralize you. So show them what you can do."

If I let myself go, I knew, I would cry for the next ten years. And, God knows, I had enough reasons to bawl.

But, when something bothers me, I eat. So I went to the village cafeteria and ate a mountain of ice cream. Then I asked for a massage.

On the day of the final, I wasn't really nervous. I looked for Mom in the stands, but I couldn't see her. I was the last to go, and while I was waiting my turn, I sort of strummed my legs. I was a little sad — no, not sad, but melancholic. I took more care doing each of my little rituals; I attended to each detail so that the memory would stay with me when everything was over. I applied gel to my hair for the last time. I would never swim again. That was decided. It didn't matter how the Games turned out, I would retire right afterward. I wanted to have a different life. I had already made that decision, with Sylvain. Now, what was left for me? But, in spite of the emptiness left inside of me by Sylvain's death, it never occurred to me to reconsider this decision.

Anyway, there were still a few minutes left in my career. Although it had knocked me for a loop, the catastrophe of the previous day had galvanized me. Before retiring, I was determined to make my mark: "You'll regret not having given me my points." Indeed, one hour before, the guillotine had fallen. The appeal had been rejected.

We had expected this. The head judge and the appeals judge were American, and so was my main rival. When we heard that not one witness had been called — not the Brazilian judge, nor the Swedish judge, who had never been generous with us but who had gone on our behalf to "obtain justice and say what had happened," nor any of the other judges who had come forward to tell their version — we understood. Even so, for the last twenty-four hours, every Canadian in the Olympic delegation had fought hard.

"I've never felt such support from Synchro Canada," Julie told me afterward. "Everyone here has made an incredible effort to reverse the decision."

The chef de mission, Ken Read, an ex-downhill skier, had fought tooth and nail, doing everything that was humanly possible. When I found out, a little later, that Dick Pound, president of the Canadian Olympic Association and vice-president of the International Olympic Committee, had rebuked him in public, I was shocked. I had the impression that Ken could not have done more. So, I said to myself, "If you think you can do it, go ahead!" Since then, Dick Pound has been taking care of the affair.

Calmly, Julie explained to me how things had happened: the appeals committee had justified its decision by saying that it had listened to the American chief judge's explanation and felt that it was sufficient. The whole thing had lasted ten minutes and required only four lines of minutes.

I had one way left to protest: to swim better than I had ever swum before, to beat the American in the final, to make them bitterly regret their decision. In short, to show the whole world who the real champion was.

My routine was much more difficult than the American's. The judges couldn't ignore this, and I would perform it with all the energy I had left. As well, the American hadn't received any 10s, so there was a little room left for me.

"I don't have much of a chance," I thought, "but at least they'll see what I'm made of."

I did win the solo routine in the Olympics, but in spite of the 10s on the board, the combination of marks wasn't enough to win the gold. In the heat of the action, I felt like I was walking on water, but when I watched the film, I found an error during the bells: when the peals reached me on the underwater speakers, my legs weren't as straight as they should have been. The routine was so difficult, much more demanding than the American's, and the judges recognized this. But it wasn't enough . . .

As they waited for me to begin the medal ceremony, I calmly wiped off a bit of the gel that was dripping onto my shoulders, I changed, I folded my swimsuit. I felt at peace with myself: I had swum well.

Those few moments spent on the second step of the podium seemed like the longest in my life. "God, will it ever end?" I thought.

While Kristen Babb paraded around the pool, proudly holding up her gold medal and lifting the American flag she had draped around her neck, I began to lose my patience. A few feet behind her, as befitted the losers, the Japanese bronze medalist and I waited for her to move forward. But Kristen was wringing her victory for every last drop. Maybe she had a tattoo to show off, too? All this ceremony was getting on my nerves. All I could think about was finding a little corner to sit in and think, all I wanted was some peace.

"Are you angry at the American?" The question kept coming back in one form or another at the press conference. I found it ridiculous. Why should I be angry with her? She had nothing to do with it. She was an athlete like me, she'd done her best, as I had, and I sincerely hoped that her victory would be the best memory of her life.

No, I wasn't angry at the Brazilian either. She had made a mistake, like anyone could. She had tried to correct it.

Above all, I didn't want this story to tarnish my sport. And for myself, all I wanted was to be left alone so that I could cry in peace.

It was the answer to the only question asked of the Japanese girl, the bronze medallist, who had gone with me into the press room after Kristen left, that moved me the most.

"What do you think about what happened to Sylvie?" a reporter asked.

The tiny, erect Japanese girl said that she admired me very much, because I had lots of courage, and I would always be an example to her.

No tribute could have touched me more.

Afterward, it seemed like I couldn't take two steps without a Canadian coming up to me and saying, "You're our champion!" I smiled, but my heart wasn't in it.

"All the same, it's a silver medal you're wearing around your neck, my girl."

The fact remained that although I'd been beating her for years, it was Kristen who had the Olympic title.

Julie took our cause to an even higher level, contesting the decision with the International Amateur Swimming Federation.

In the end, I told myself, whatever their decision, I would

always feel like something had been stolen from me. I would never have the experience of standing with my arms in the air on the Olympic podium, hearing my national anthem. Anyway, if the Federation awarded me my gold medal, how would they do it? Send it by courier?

Still, I knew that some people were even unhappier than I was when I saw Chris Johnson's disconsolate face on television. I had met him for the first time at the 1990 Commonwealth Games in New Zealand. Like his brother, Greg, he was a boxer. At first, I thought he was crazy.

"Sylvie, I recognize your legs."

He looked a little like Bill Cosby, but a Bill Cosby with a Phentex cap, which gave him a slightly delinquent air. One day, in the middle of the bus, he began to pretend he was taking pictures of my legs. I found the situation ridiculous and didn't really know how to react. And then, I had my prejudices. After all, he was a boxer . . .

Later, he and his brother sometimes came to cheer us on at the Claude-Robillard Centre. No, Chris wasn't crazy: he was a clown.

While he got his ticket to the Barcelona Games, his brother Greg didn't manage to qualify. Chris had sworn to win for Greg.

His bronze medal around his neck, in front of the television cameras, he cried hot tears: "I'm sorry, Greg!"

He was crying not for himself, but for his brother, to whom he wouldn't be bringing home the promised gold medal. When I heard that some thought he was a complainer, it hurt me.

That evening, I saw him and I tried to comfort him. "Chris, you have a medal. Be proud." But he didn't react.

In spite of everything that had happened to me, I wasn't sad, as he was. I had my pride. In fact, rather than feeling sad, I was really suffering from acute heartsickness. Now I had the right to say, "Leave me in peace." Finally, I had the right to cry. And I wanted to go home and burrow under the covers, with my toys . . .

All my life, I'd been surrounded by toys. When people made fun of Nadia because she picked up her doll after her Olympic performance in Montreal, I remember that it hurt me. I never went anywhere without my stuffed toy. Even at the world championships, in January of 1991, I slept with my Garfield. I wanted to be with my cats and my toys again. Now that I was finished with synchronized swimming, that was almost all that was left of my life.

The day after the solo final, the Vilagos twins also won a silver medal. It was a true achievement, considering that they had been retired for five years, an achievement that would have made a much bigger splash if all these tragedies hadn't befallen me and monopolized the media attention.

That evening was completely mad and didn't end until the wee hours of the morning. Radio stations from all over the place had left messages. Sometimes, when I introduced myself or waited for another call from a listener, I was put on hold and I could listen to the program on the air.

"All mothers dream of having a daughter like her," said one listener.

I found that funny. "There! Mom should hear that. And Martin always thought I was such a rotten character."

I didn't understand. They were talking about me so much, it was incredible, but in such terms . . . Everyone seemed to find it admirable that I had turned up for the medal presentation, that I had agreed to step onto the podium. Was I hearing right? For me, it was natural to turn up. I had never stopped to consider such a thing for a moment; it had never occurred to me not to go. Never.

After a multitude of interviews, I spoke, on live television, to my grandmother and my whole band of crazies.

Since the Brazilian judge's mistake, almost no one mentioned Sylvain's suicide anymore. One might have thought that this new tragedy had somehow erased the previous one, which was still so recent. I had suddenly gone from being a victim to being the girl who hadn't given up.

They talked about courage, but I was so scared: "What will happen to me? Karine, what will I do?"

SIXTEEN

The Whirlpool

"Sylvie! Sylvie! Sylvie!"

It was after midnight, but with the time difference, for me it was almost dawn. Sleep, I would give anything to sleep.

But when I saw the crowd gathered at the Dorval airport, I had a new rush of adrenalin. And I had thought that because I had won only the silver medal, the welcome would be lukewarm . . .

Just before I left Barcelona, I was in touch with National and Daniel Lamarre. I desperately needed someone to help me. Daniel tried to prepare me: "There's Sylvie Fréchette fever here. It will be big, so get ready."

Martin had also tried to get the message to me. With Mom, Julie, and me in Barcelona, he was left to hold down the fort in Montreal, and the telephone was ringing off the hook. One radio station had called at six o'clock one morning, waking him up, and asked him his reaction to the story of the Brazilian judge, which he didn't even know about yet. Poor Martin! He is one of those people who needs at least an hour after he wakes up to turn into a human being, and in the meantime, he's in a murderous mood, as grouchy as an unfed bear. All his life, no one ever dared talk to him when he woke up, for fear that he would send all the saints in heaven after us.

When he suggested that I prepare for the worst, I thought that he had, like Daniel Lamarre, lost his mind. "But you're completely nuts," I protested.

I didn't believe them, I couldn't believe them. After all, I had only won the silver medal.

Bombardier had chartered a private jet to take us from Toronto to Dorval, and I made the trip in the cockpit, between the two pilots. If I had been a little less tired, less of a zombie, this unusually favourable treatment might have tipped me off. But, no!

When I arrived at Dorval, I was in shock. The crowd was chanting my name. From the sea of bouncing Brita placards, they threw me dolphins. RCMP officers pushed back the crowd to keep me from being crushed. One would have thought that I was the pope on an official visit.

A motorized cart carried me toward a sort of stage, where Jean-Luc Mongrain, Lise Payette, and Yves Létourneau presented me with a huge twenty-four-carat gold medal, in the shape of a dolphin, cast by Noranda Mines. "This is from all of Quebec," they told me.

Never in my life would I have believed that they loved me so much. A handicapped little girl had even gotten a temporary leave from the hospital to come see me. The welcome and the gold-medal presentation were broadcast live by TVA and CKAC.

After the television reporters came the print journalists.

"Now, I want to step back a little," I told them, "put a little order in my life, come back to earth, and see what I want to do in the future."

I was exhausted. When they asked me if I was satisfied, I felt like I was dodging the issue: "I swam with my heart. I wanted to give the performance of my life, and I did. And so I'm happy."

It was more than I could stand. I found the welcome very, very nice, but I could think only of going to bed.

"Could you repeat that in English?"

A little after two o'clock, things calmed down, and we were finally able to leave the airport. A bus driver had made Martin an offer to take the whole family for free, and we drove to Grandma's crowded together and singing.

At five-thirty, we finally got to Jean-Pierre's, where I had just a few hours to sleep. I was expected at National at eleven o'clock for a series of interviews, and the party was just starting.

In the next few weeks, I felt like I was caught up in a tornado.

"Sylvie, the prime minister is calling for you."

"Oh, sure, and Pope John Paul II is on hold."

But it was him. At the other end of the line, Mr. Mulroney called me Sylvie as he congratulated me.

The next day, in the *Journal de Montréal* parking lot, a radio program organized in my honour drew a huge crowd. I heard, through my earphones, famous Quebecers thanking me: Luc de Larochellière, Marie-Denise Pelletier, Michel Rivard, Montreal mayor Jean Doré and his Laval counterpart, Gilles Vaillancourt, Pierre Harvey, Sylvie Bernier, Gaétan Boucher, Myriam Bédard, and many more.

But thanks for what, good God! For doing what I love for eighteen years?

It seemed like pure fantasy that so many people had come to see me. I was literally floating on a cloud, incredulous and overwhelmed. There were medals, trophies, invitations to give talks, even love letters — no end of them.

The Expos invited me and other athletes from the Games to the Olympic Stadium. When I was introduced and I heard the crowd yelling, my heart skipped a beat. I couldn't even breathe.

Invited to drop the puck for the ceremonial face-off at a

Nordiques game, I felt the same way. The spectators stood up; as I went off the ice, the seats made a "toc toc toc" noise. I felt like my heart was beating to the same rhythm.

Each time, I had the same shiver . . .

Listing all the honours would be long and pretentious. So I'll mention just one more, the one that touched me the most. It was a spring evening, and the Canadian Sports Awards were being given out. Up for the award were Kerrin Lee-Gartner, Olympic gold medallist in downhill skiing, Silken Laumann, who had set an example in Olympic courage and determination a few months after a terrible injury by earning a bronze medal in rowing when her very presence at the Olympics was a miracle, and me. The award went to Kerrin, but Silken would have deserved it just as much.

Suddenly, Minister Pierrre Cadieux announced that a new trophy would be awarded from now on to athletes who kept their pride and dignity in the face of adversity. The trophy would be named after . . . Sylvie Fréchette.

Daniel Lamarre, who was sitting beside me and to whom the news was also a surprise, grabbed my arm. For a moment, I thought his fingers would leave a permanent imprint in my flesh. Then, trembling, taken by surprise, I stood up. I would be the first to receive the trophy in my name.

As I moved toward the stage, I was thinking of only one thing: where to put my feet, which were shaking in my high heels.

I had no idea of what to say. All I know is that I cried for a long time . . . in both French and English.

The trophy wasn't very big, but it meant that I deserved to be remembered. It was a way of making a place for me in history. One day, in twenty, thirty, or fifty years, the trophy will be handed to an athlete who will ask, "Who was Sylvie Fréchette?" And someone will tell him or her . . .

When I got back to Quebec, I had various offers to work in public relations. On the advice of National, I finally chose the most interesting, and so I became the National Bank's spokesperson.

It was interesting, and not just in terms of remuneration. The president of the bank, André Bérard, told me, "I would be happy to have you represent us, but we don't want you to go away empty-handed." So he offered me not only a sponsorship, but training. Me, who knew absolutely nothing about the business world, and who hadn't finished my bachelor's degree; after eighteen years of training, I didn't know how to do much but swim. That's what decided me.

I found my desire to exchange information, to push forward, answered by Nicole Rondou, who took the rookie in hand.

At chambers of commerce, schools, and other places, I told my story. And they asked again. And again and again.

From time to time, I was asked about the Olympics or Sylvain's death. But more often, they asked me to talk about my training. And so I told them about the empty Javex bottles that helped us to float with our heads underwater and to feel all of our muscles without being obsessed with our arm movements and the pain they caused. When our arms were "on holiday," we could feel our muscles contract and recognize the ones that should be working.

I also talked about the lengths we swam in every stroke — crawl, back stroke, breast stroke, and butterfly — just like "real" swimmers. Except that, in synchronized swimming, we swam in the afternoon or evening, never the morning. As well, like other disciplines, synchronized swimming had something to teach others. Did you know that Olympic champion swimmer Mark Tewksbury worked with Debbie Muir, a synchronized-swimming coach, to correct a few little hitches in his stroke?

There was also the tubing. This was exactly the opposite of the Javex bottles. Julie had discovered the horrible yellow rubber tubes in a hospital. What they were used for there, I have no idea, but they were a daily instrument of torture for us. We put them around our waist, and when we did the "egg-beater," the rotational leg movements that kept us on the surface without using our arms, the seven extra kilograms weighed us down. When we went to competitions, we felt so light . . .

From time to time, we swam in leotards to make us heavier. There were also flexibility exercises and, of course, bodybuilding . . . In short, I explained everything.

Whenever I arrived in their region, the National Bank managers had a big smile for me. I learned quickly to recognize that smile. It always preceded a sentence that went something like, "I hope you're well rested. You have a big day ahead of you." The previous day, I had handed out synchronized-swimming awards before going to Toronto. The day before that, I had visited a school.

I loved simply talking with people — much more, in fact, than making formal speeches — just being there, chatting and answering questions. With young people, that's the way it often happened. Most of the time, the teachers chose the most deserving students. Whether it was my presence or just the break in routine that was really the gift and excited them so, I don't know. But the most absurd questions sometimes sprang up.

One day, I visited a huge school, with both elementary and secondary classes. This time, I would be talking to the older children. As I waited for them to file into the gymnasium where I was to speak, a class of second-graders passed nearby. A little boy recognized me, and obviously very cheeky, came forward:

"Hey, Sylvie Fréchette!"

"Hello, what's your name?"

"I'm Daniel. Hey, Sylvie Fréchette, how old are you?"

"Daniel, how old do you think I am?"

I think he took the question as a challenge. He began to

mull things over as he inspected me from head to foot for a long time — too long for my taste.

Then came his answer: "Forty-eight!"

I wanted to die. Me and my big mouth!

Of course, someone asked the same question in the gym.

"This time, I won't let you guess. I'll tell you straight out." And I told the story of Daniel, happy to avoid the same kind of indignity.

Once, in a high school in Dollard-des-Ormeaux or Beaconsfield, a special class of potential dropouts was invited to meet me. Perhaps I could motivate them a little, their teachers told me. My God! I didn't know exactly what to say, and I had no idea how they would react. For lack of something better, I decided to talk to them very simply.

Synchronized swimming lit up my youth, as it does many little girls' lives. So, as usual, I wanted to tell them about the girls who still joyfully came to the pool — my little worms, as I called them. And then it came out, clear and well articulated:

"The pack of little whores . . ."

In front of me, the young people froze, smiling.

Near the door were the teacher, the principal, and the people from the bank. I wanted to disappear, to drop through the floor. What would they say?

Very slowly, I turned around: they were laughing like crazy, so I burst out laughing, too. As for the young people, they gave me a standing ovation.

But it didn't matter, I wasn't asked back. From then on, when I came to this part, I articulated very carefully: worms. They could have given me a prize for pronuncation. And I'd pick a peck of pickled peppers!

And there were other sticky situations. For example, I've always been very expressive with my hands. It wasn't unusual for my long arms to knock over a glass in a restaurant. I'd excuse myself quietly and politely, and move on to something else. The problem now was that I often found myself in the place of honour.

Once, while I was on tour with the bank in Laval, I was at a luncheon. Of course, I was seated at the head table, which everyone watched like hawks. Everything went fine until dessert. On the plate before me was a beautiful pear, standing like a soldier at attention, with raspberry sauce flowing down its shoulders. Since I was the guest, the others waited until I began before they dug in. I took my fork, and . . . the pear went flying. Splash! The tablecloth all around me was red.

"It's not serious . . . It's not serious."

The more they said this, the deeper I blushed.

Later, as I toured the tables to say good evening to everyone, I noticed with relief the many raspberry-coloured stains decorating the tablecloths. If I ever serve pears for dessert, I'll make sure they're well cooked.

"Tomorrow, Sylvie, you have a press conference, then there's a speech at the Optimists Club. Oh, yes, and you mustn't forget to call Toronto. Aside from that, there's a request for a telethon, and a fundraiser . . ."

Three or four meetings per day, seven days a week. And, to please everyone, I would have had to be in three places at the same time. Fortunately, Daniel Lamarre was there to say no for me.

And I had thought that people who weren't synchronized swimmers had the right to a day off . . .

After a while, I was having the same horrible sensation that I thought had gone forever: the synchronized swimmer's panic of the last few seconds. I no longer had the time to breathe. "Go on, girl, dive again. You can do it. It's almost over!"

SEVENTEEN

And Now?

June 1993. Ten months later.

I told myself that things would calm down with time, but they haven't! However, I've managed to build a little wall around myself, and for the first time in my life, I can say no sometimes, even to Daniel Lamarre, even to the bank.

No doubt, it's Karine who's giving me this courage. But I can even send her packing more often than she would want. "Leave me alone," I tell her, "I want to be just Sylvie."

It's not always easy to be just Sylvie.

"Now, you can eat chocolate cookies . . ."

In the supermarket, a man looked into my cart and smiled. He was being friendly, not mean at all, but I felt like I'd been caught in the act.

"I know, it's true, I like to eat a lot. I've gained two kilos since the Games . . ."

If I could have, I would have left the man and the cart right there and I would have run out of the grocery store. I felt ridiculous, not just because of the cookies, but because of my reaction. What was happening to me?

After all, I laughed at my little binges, too. "You know,

Mom, I even have a little belly. Look at this. I've never had a belly before . . ."

For the first time, I thought I saw some cellulite as I was getting into the shower. I laughed: "Now you're a true woman, my girl."

It felt funny to go from being a little crazy to being normal. In fact, "normal" meant a lot of things.

It was almost impossible for me to go to a store, a movie, or a restaurant without being recognized. One time, Mom and I thought we had succeeded. Oh, we had put luck on our side by sitting in a rather dark alcove, and I had my back to the room. No one came over or even looked at us. We had mischievous smiles of victory on our faces . . . until the waiters came forward with a lovely cake: "Dear Sylvie, it's your turn . . ."

It was so sweet! It's strange: for years, I was unknown. Now that people recognize me, there are times when I'd like to go back, even just for a couple of hours, to the time when no one knew who I was except Mom and my family. But I know very well that if that happened, I would regret it, and I would miss all of this human warmth and love terribly. The one they recognize is Karine, I know, not Sylvie. But Sylvie's had enough of Karine.

In fact, Karine scares me a little: What if it's just Karine people like, not Sylvie! Oh, it's so complicated. And yet, in the end, it's simple: I'd like to be famous one day out of two: Karine one day, Sylvie the next.

Here and there, I've also managed to find quiet moments to myself. One time, I was sitting in a lawn chair, watching the sunset on the back balcony of my house. I had bought myself another house, in Laval. It's nothing like the dream house that Sylvain had found for us. But it's big, light, and all white. On the wall of my bedroom is a neon artpiece of a wave. Elsewhere, there are Garfield posters. But, no! God, no! Absolutely no medals. They're still all at Mom's, on the curtain rod.

For a few months, I stayed at Jean-Pierre's place with Mom. When I got home, my supper was ready. I lived in a cocoon; sometimes, I wanted to slip into a sweat suit and just nibble something a few hours later, or even not eat at all. For four months, I was surrounded with love and affection, enveloped in well-being. But I felt too good. I wanted to have some difficulties, to be independent.

So that's how I found myself in my new house, alone with my four cats. But although I needed some time alone, I was scared of it, too. It was when I was alone that I had flashbacks.

After the Games, I had to go back to the apartment several times. I could never do it unless I took a gang of people with me, as if to protect myself from my ghosts and my memories.

One day, as I emptied my grocery bags, I noticed the box of cereal. *He* was the one who ate this cereal, not me. But I couldn't ever throw it out. I couldn't listen to the music we liked, but I could never throw out those cassettes either. For months, I couldn't even watch RDS.

The most difficult thing was everyday life. I still have so many questions that haven't been answered, that will never be answered.

The other day was Sylvain's birthday. I thought about him all day. How would I manage to live through July 18? I wanted to sleep, without nightmares, and wake up three days later. Cross the damned day off the calendar, like the hotel owners who don't have a thirteenth floor.

People said all sorts of things about Sylvain and me: that he committed suicide because I was thinking about leaving him, because I had a lover, because, because . . . In restaurants, people began to look at Martin worriedly. And they said that Sylvain had killed himself to hurt me, to ruin my Games.

That's ridiculous. Sylvain always wanted the best for me. I'll never believe that he wanted to hurt me. I don't want to believe it. I don't know why he did it. But now I have to accept that the questions will remain unanswered, for me as well as everyone else.

When I got back from the Games, daily life was hell. During the day, I was as strong as Samson, since the whirlpool kept me from thinking, but at night, I cried in bed.

"You big hypocrite! So tell them that you're in pain." But I was scared to show it, as though the pain would get worse if I admitted its existence.

In my diary, I wrote, "Today, instead of lying, I'd rather not write."

Even today, it's difficult for me to see Jennifer, Josée's daughter and Sylvain's niece. She's also my niece, our niece. She hasn't forgotten either. At first, every time I saw her she'd present me with a riddle. It was a well-rehearsed story, and she'd give both the questions and the answers.

"Guess what I'm thinking of. A star."

I didn't have to hear the rest. I already knew it.

"Do you know who's in the star?"

Yes, yes, I knew who was in the star.

"It's Sylvain . . ."

I still haven't gone to the cemetery. Right after the Games, I didn't think I could. Then I had the excuse of winter. It was cold and dark; I wanted to wait until spring. So, what's stopping me now?

I'm scared of traffic jams. Of course, everyone hates them. But when I'm stuck in one, the smell of exhaust comes back to me. Then, before I can do anything, it surrounds me and takes me to hell.

In the spring, I managed to take a week's vacation. I was exhausted and wanted to go somewhere without twelve swim-suits and my nose plugs.

The travel agent spoke glowingly of the Turks and Caicos Islands and told me that there was a dolphin there who sometimes swam with the tourists, especially women. He would like me, I was sure.

But the dolphin didn't come that week. The sea was the turquoise that gave the islands their name. Paradise. Happy finally to meet someone who could hold her breath long enough to dive with him, the guide took me into caverns to admire the multicoloured fish and the coral. Wow!

The beach, soft and white, was magnificent. My mind was empty, but I felt good. On the sand was a chaise longue that someone had pulled there, leaving two clean parallel lines. Like the stretcher on the carpet in the condo. Oh, no, not that! Not here!

Even in paradise, I couldn't escape.

For months, I couldn't confide in my diary. Oh, I wrote all the time, come rain or come shine. Each time, I began with a cold hello. But the Little Prince had disappeared.

In November, he came back. One evening, either in the bath or in my bed, I wrote, "Good night, Little Prince! Someone, I don't know who, but a little prince in a tall crystal tower, all sunlit, full of soft and tender colours . . . a little prince, just for me.

"Happily, I can dream. It feels good to get away from the hard reality. I've had, and still have, much too much pain to think that one day it could happen again . . ."

Ring!

I didn't answer the phone at first. I didn't want to have to refuse an invitation, to say, "I don't have the time." When it was Mom, she warned me by saying to the answering machine, "My girl, pick up the phone. It's me."

I hate saying no, especially to my girlfriends. I feel stupid saying, over and over, "I can't talk too long, I have this or that to do." I would so much like to see them. Next week, or the one after, I'll no doubt have some time to myself.

I had just moved when the phone rang. It was Caro, one of the Doré twins, friends from high school.

"What am I doing? I'm cleaning up. I've just moved, and there's mud everywhere."

"If you like, we can come and help."

I said no, I was doing all right, thanks anyway. A few minutes later, the doorbell rang. It was the twins, with a mop, a pail, and everything we needed. How could I turn down such kindness, such friendship?

Although I want to spend time with my family and friends, I also want to do all sorts of things: take a photography course and learn how to develop film, talk to my plants, roll in the snow, travel, listen to quiet music with my cats. I've missed a whole bunch of things. I can still catch up on them, but I'll have to hurry. I want to enjoy every second.

Since I got back from vacation, I've come to like diving into crowds again. I enjoy every moment of the handshakes and applause, even spending hours signing autographs. I've always preferred to talk to people plainly, as if they were old friends, so why not? There's a wicked pain in my hand that comes back from time to time. At first, they thought it was arthritis, but it isn't. So what is it? These days, I have to say no, but I don't know if people understand.

After the Olympics, I promised myself I would spend all my birthdays at home. However, this June 27 I again found myself far from home, for the closing ceremony of the Acadia Games, in Dieppe, New Brunswick. I was a little sorry that I'd accepted this invitation. Otherwise, I would have celebrated my birthday with my family for once. I was in the VIP room when suddenly Renelle, who was to sing the national anthem, intoned, "My dear Sylvie . . ." A little later, in the afternoon, we were waiting for Radio-Canada to go on the air when all the young people in the sports centre, informed I don't know how, spontaneously began to sing, "Happy Birthday, Dear Sylvie." For a moment, I thought my heart would burst. People so welcoming, all this warmth, I couldn't have had a better birthday.

Now, I'm also more interested in learning the banking business. Karine, I know, would do well in the business world.

The bank, Brita, the new line of swimsuits in my name, she would know how to navigate through all this. In fact, she's the one who helps me to speak.

Recently, I was to be interviewed on Lise Payette's program. Ms. Payette scared me. She always knew how to get the most intimate details out of her guests, digging deep . . . I accepted, but my mind was made up: it was Karine who would meet with her. Sylvie would be eaten alive. In the end, the program was cancelled at the last minute. The duel between Karine and Ms. Payette never took place.

Inevitably, every time I face the public, every time I approach a microphone, I feel the room spinning and my knees get weak. Then Karine talks to me, as she used to before every competition: "Go on, girl." And so I dive in. Once I'm in the water and under way, everything is fine.

It's strange, but even now I can't stay away from the pool, from the water. Every once in a while, I go swimming for the sheer pleasure of feeling the water on my skin, for the simple pleasure of the effort.

I think this pleasure will always be there. In Barbados, I met an old synchronized swimmer, Edmée Martineau. She must have been seventy-five, but she was graceful and delicate when she swam the crawl. Like a little girl, she showed off by doing some water ballet for me, and when I looked at her beautiful, firm legs, I found myself hoping that I'll be like her when I'm her age.

I still haven't completely given up on synchronized swimming. I have only one regret: I'm convinced that I never reached my full potential. I could have accomplished more, I know it. But I still have some good ideas. I was asked to choreograph a short routine for the national team qualifications. For an hour and a half, I found myself with my coach, in the pool I've always known, in my own element, my world, exactly as I've always wanted it. For an hour and a half, Karine and I were together, like before. It felt so good to be creative again. It felt great!

I think that creativity is what's missing. For the moment, I feel like I'm being carried on a wave . . .

Sometimes, I'm asked to give a performance, but I don't want to. It's not out of bad will, it's something else. Respect, no doubt. I don't train anymore and I'm no longer an Olympic-calibre athlete. How could I swim in front of athletes who are still at that level? How could I present a routine that doesn't match their abilities?

Choose, for example, Lisa Alexander, or another from among the best. I'll be there to cheer them on.

I don't want to live in the shadow of "Sylvie Fréchette" anymore. I don't want to live in Karine's shadow. I want her to go away. For a while.

But I know that she'll always be there for me, when I need her.